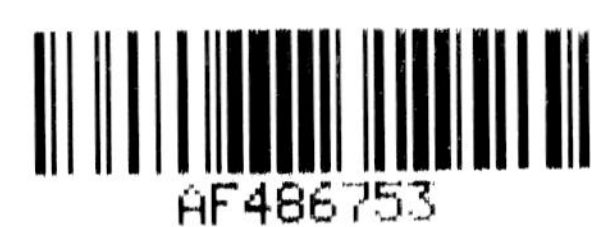


# Girl's Dream: Volume 1

## by Lovink

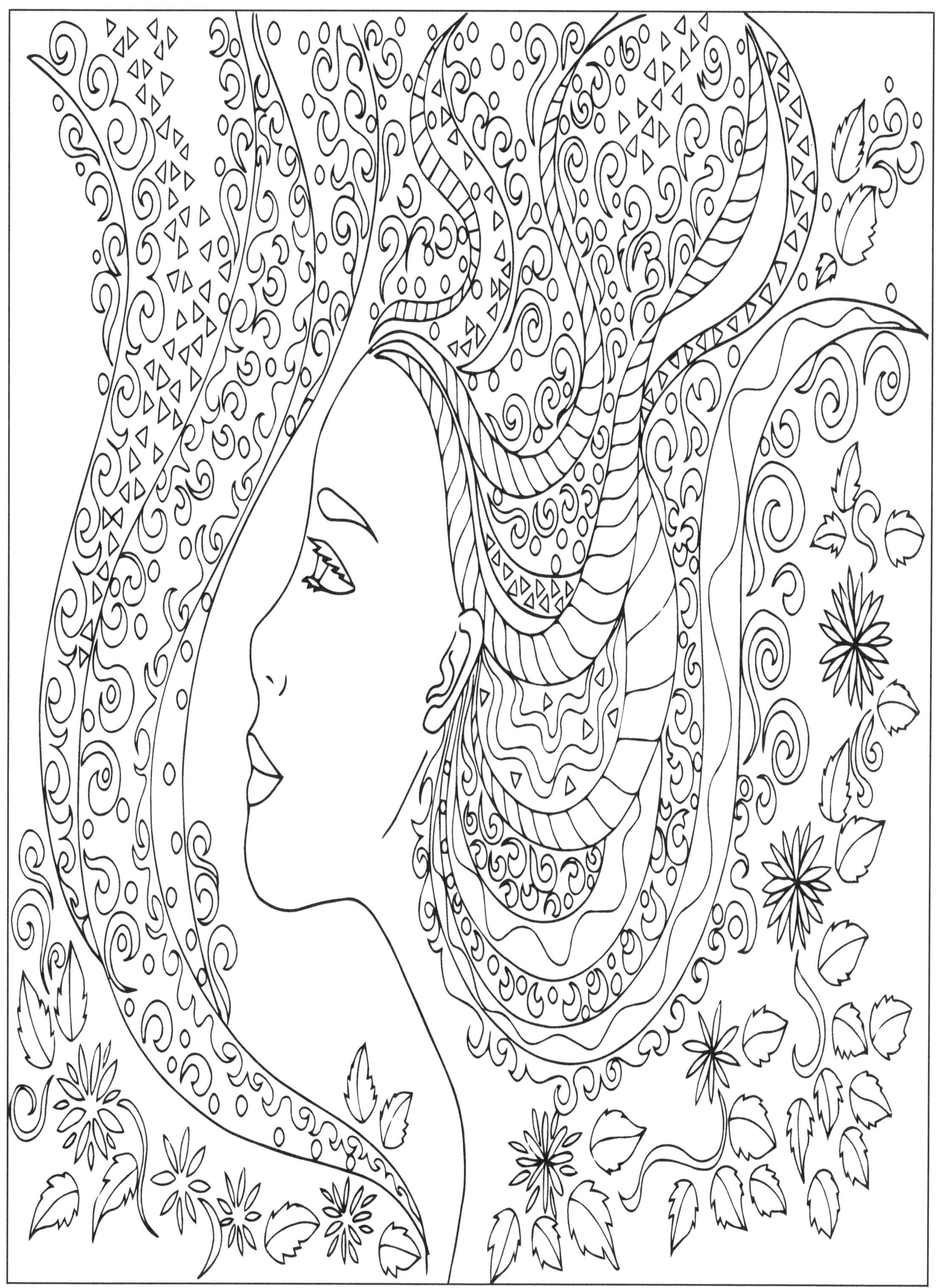

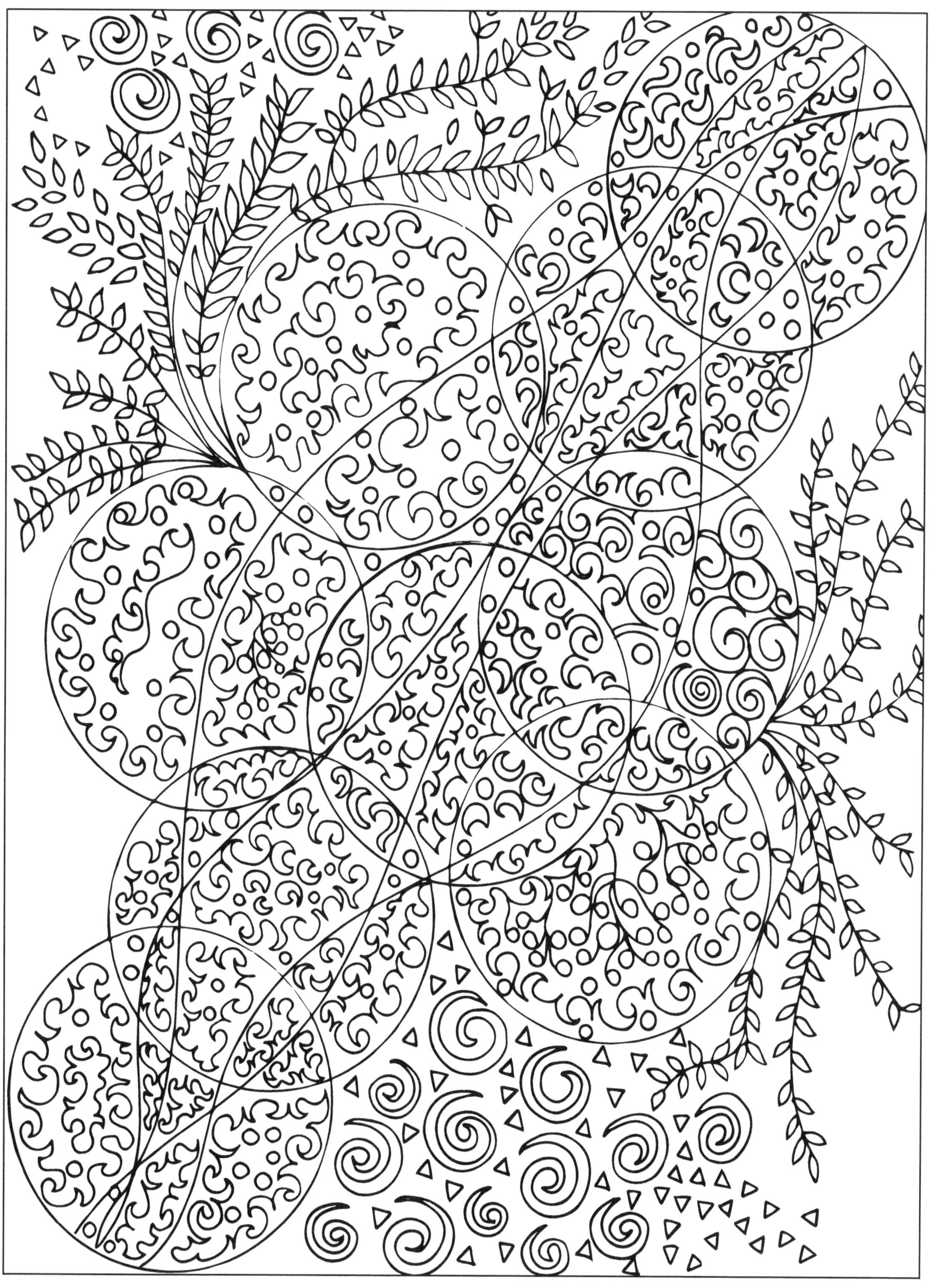

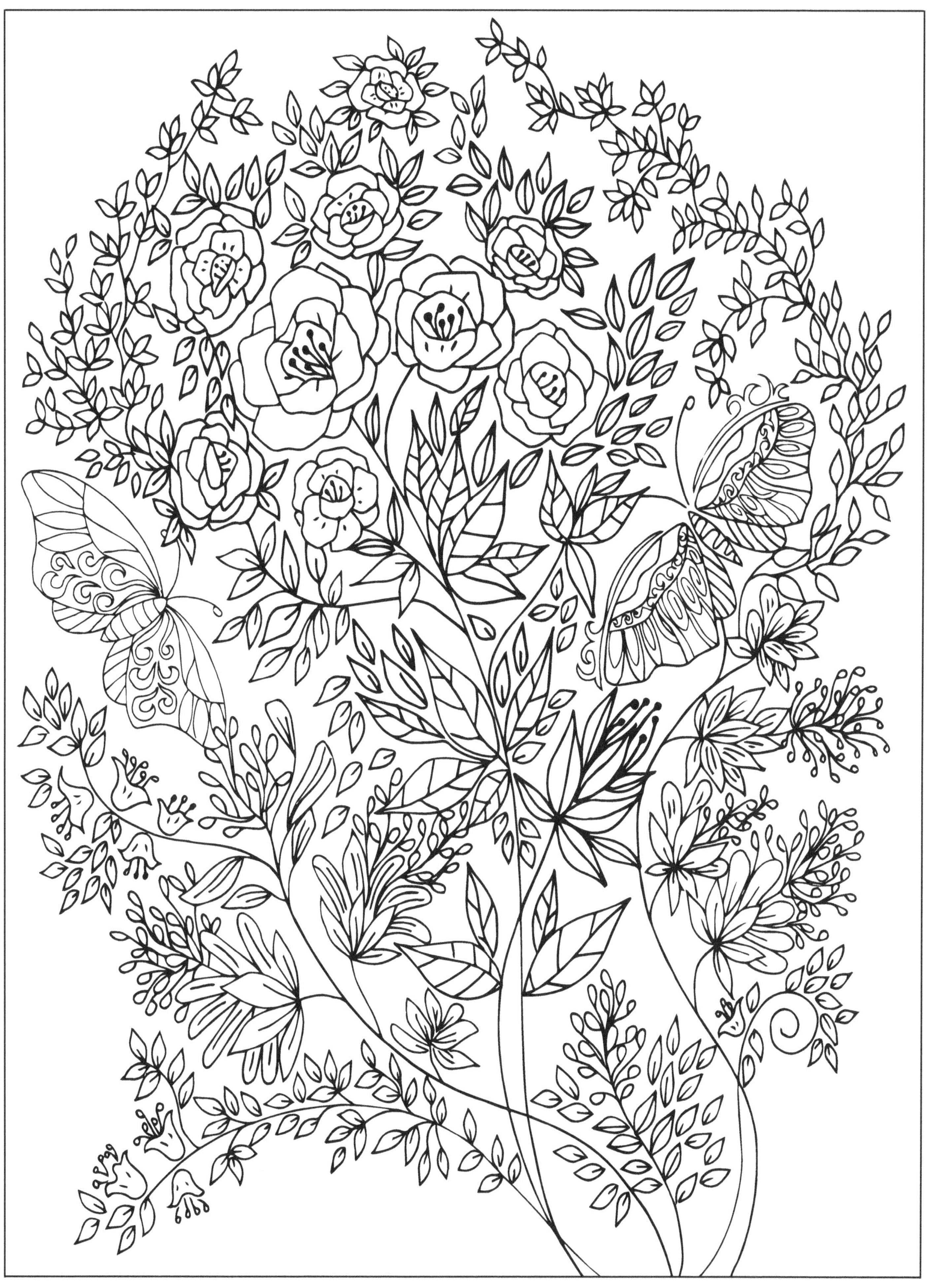

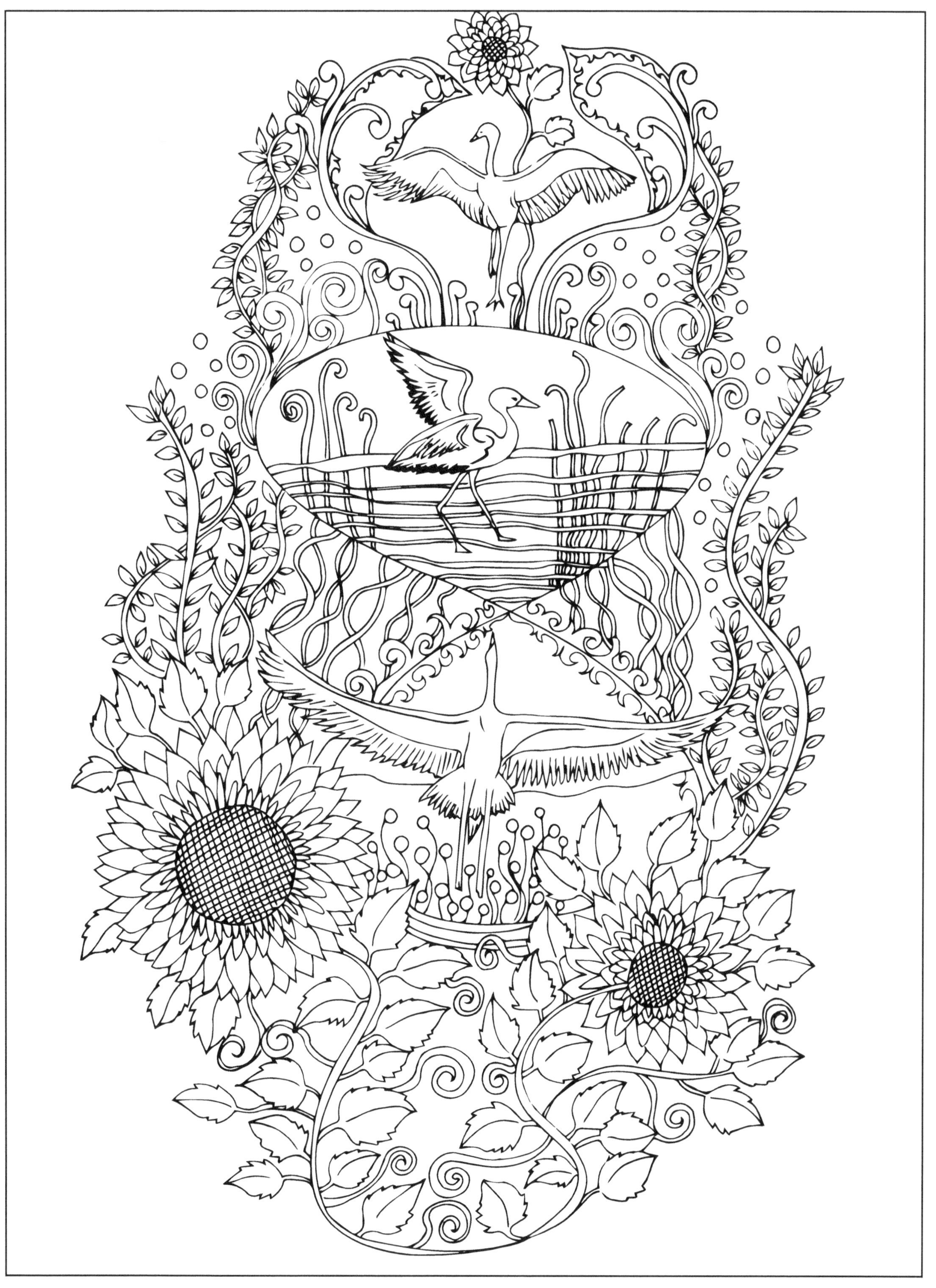

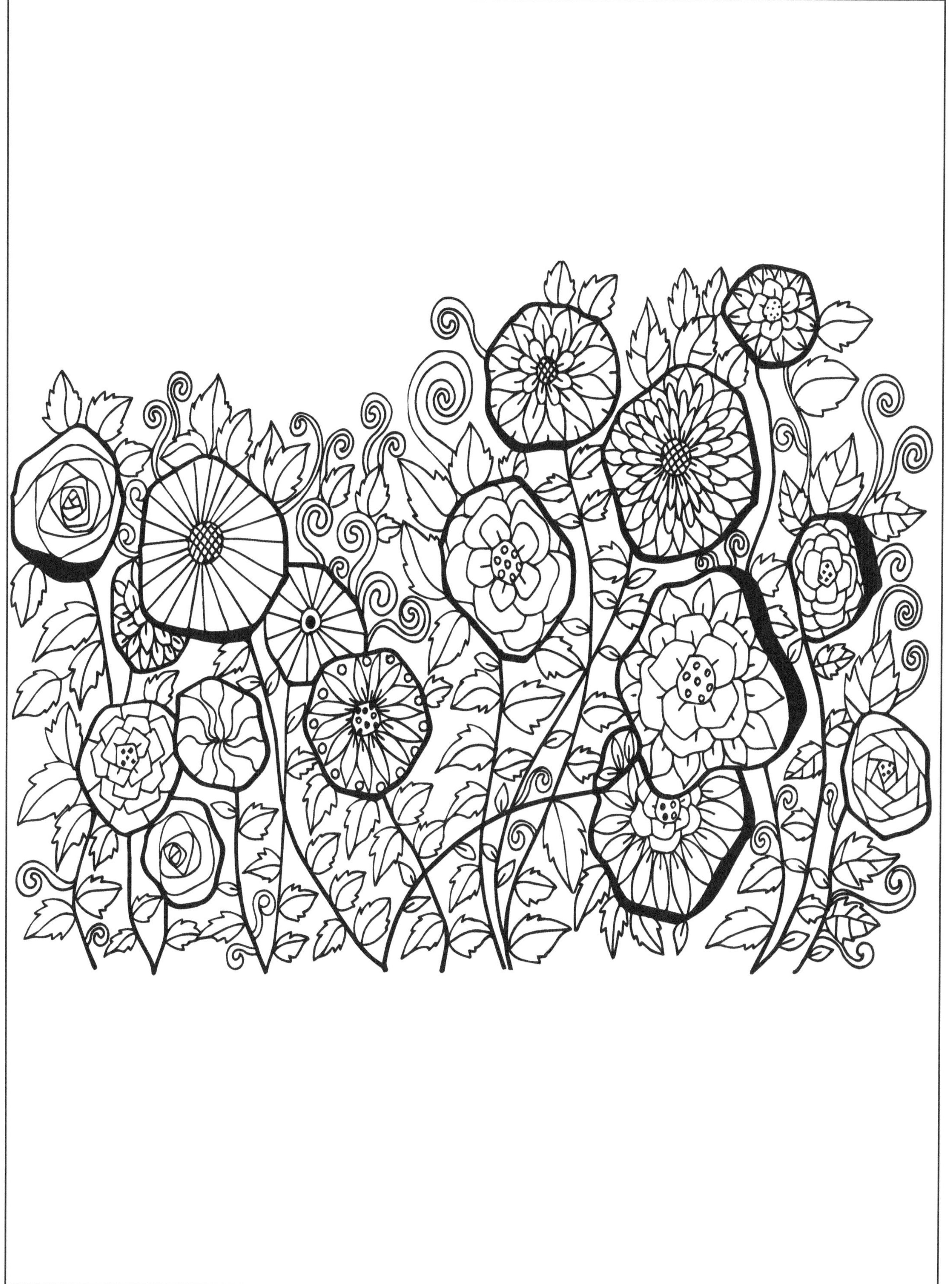

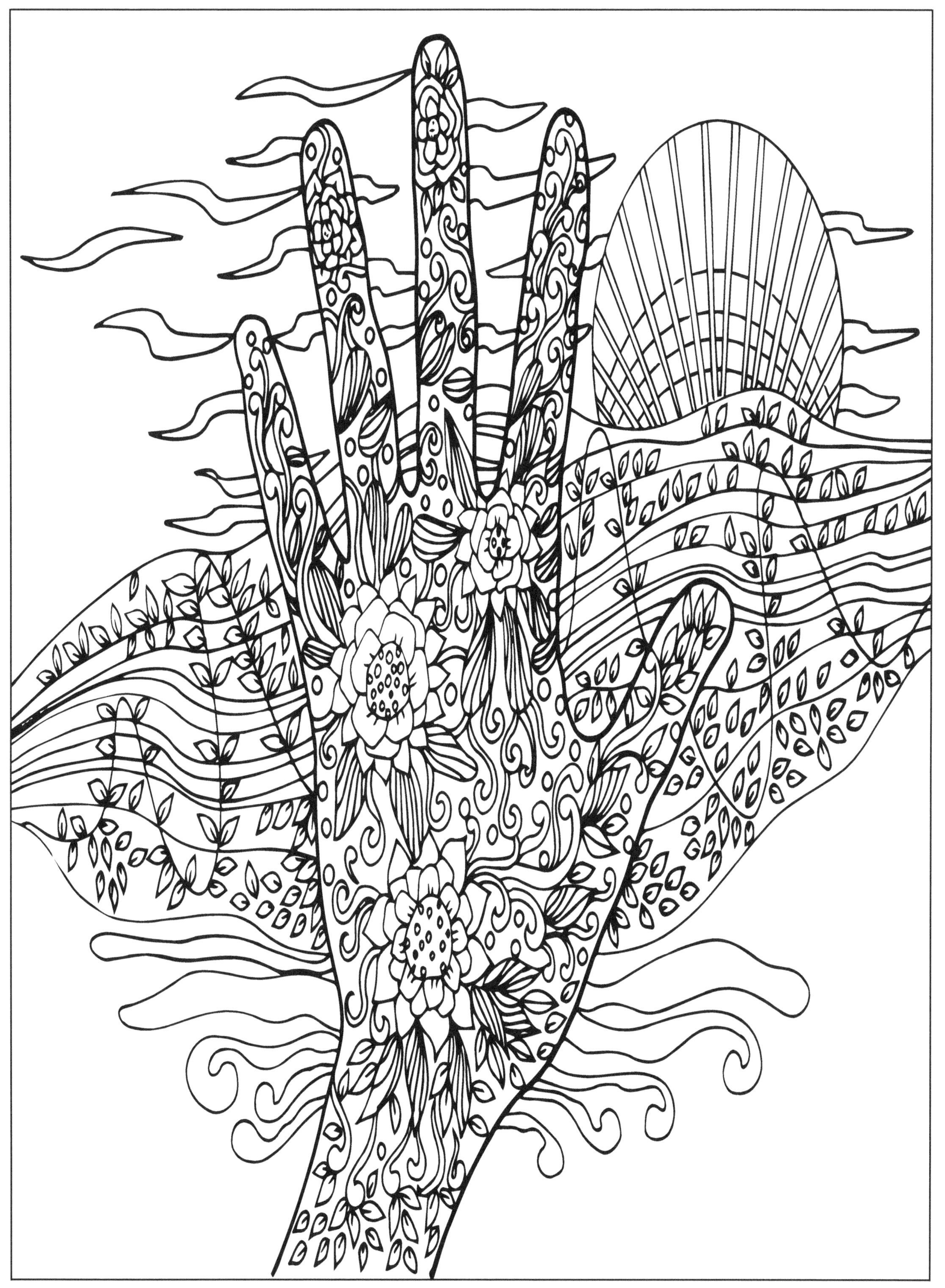

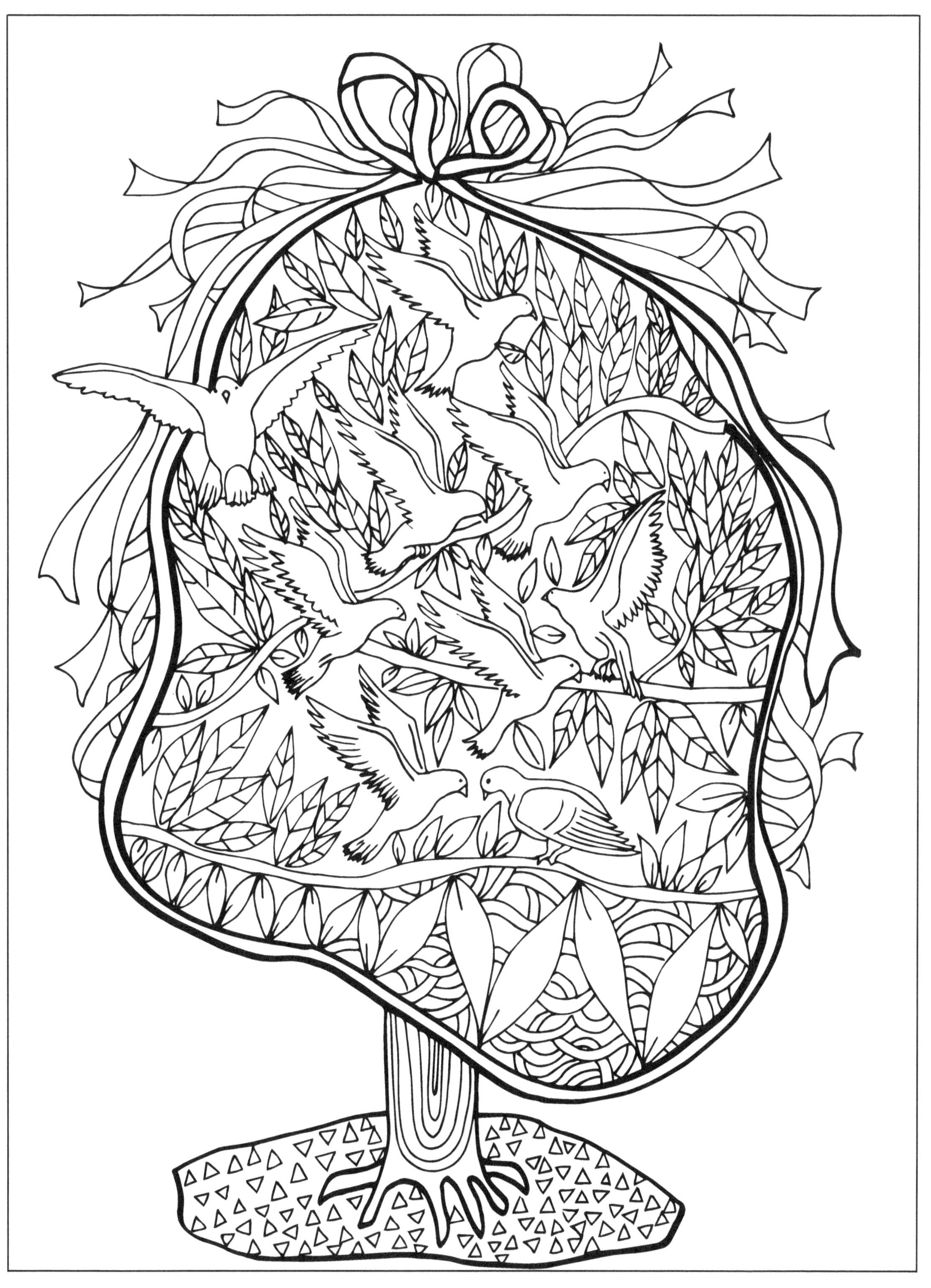

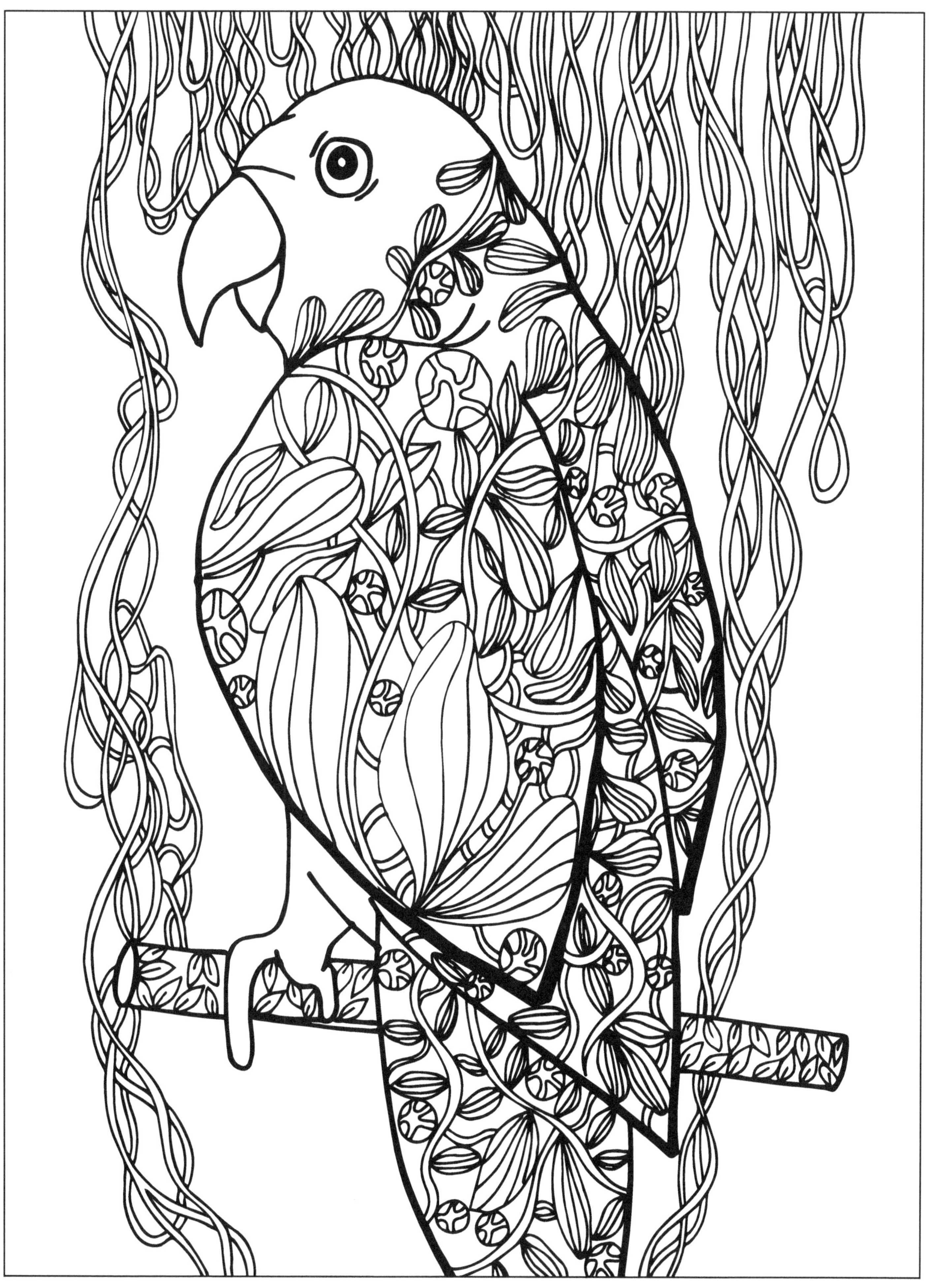

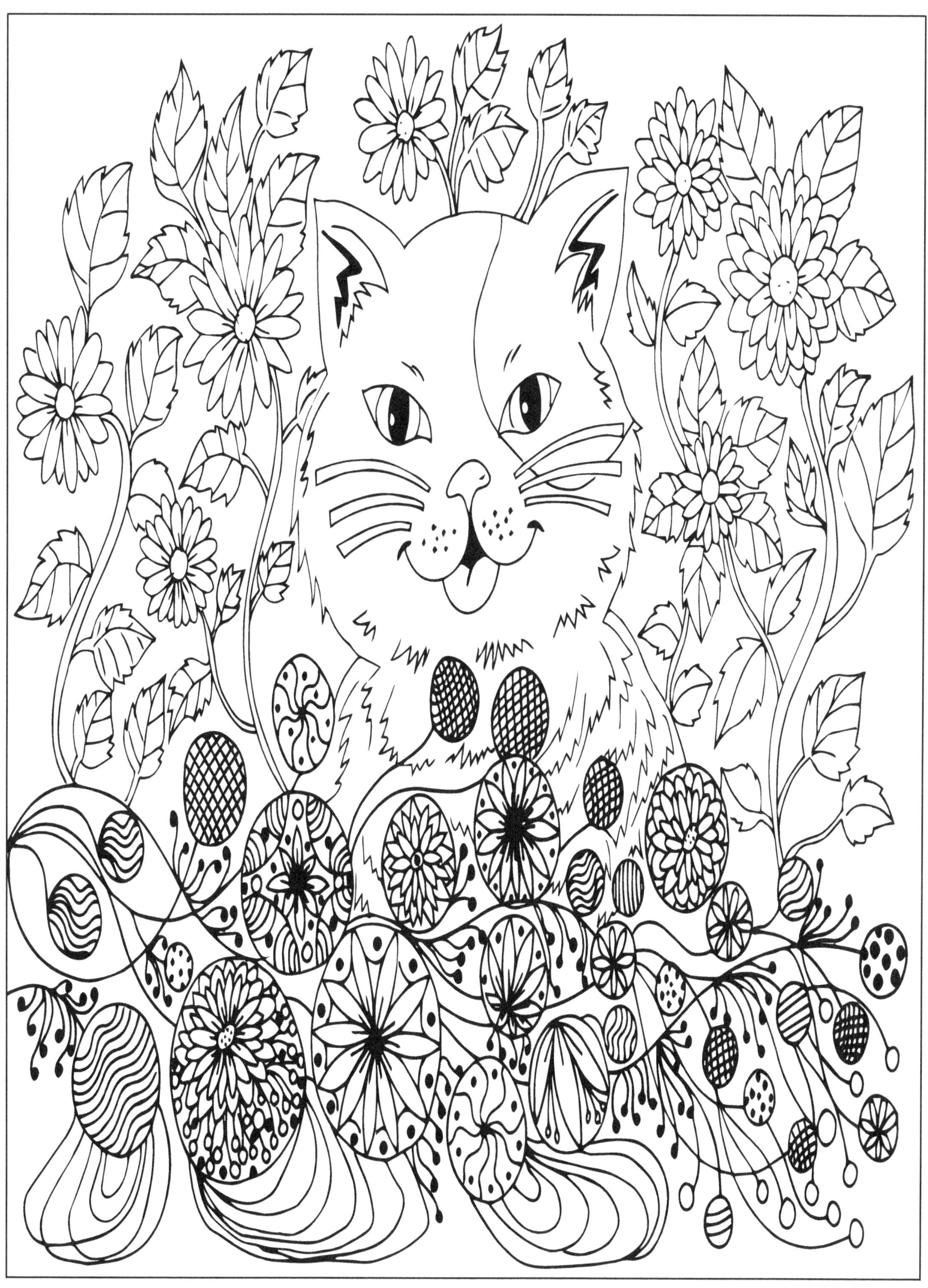

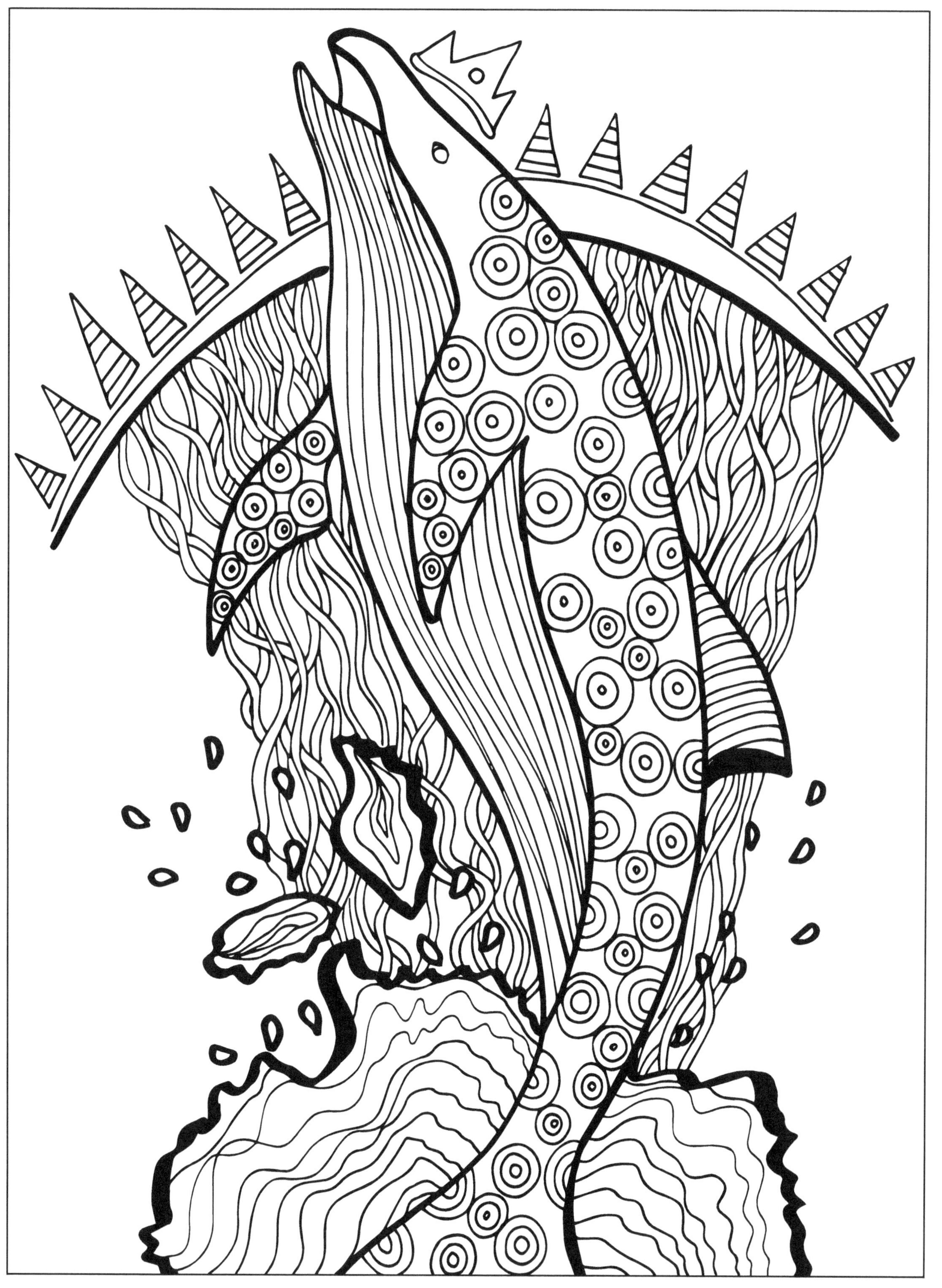

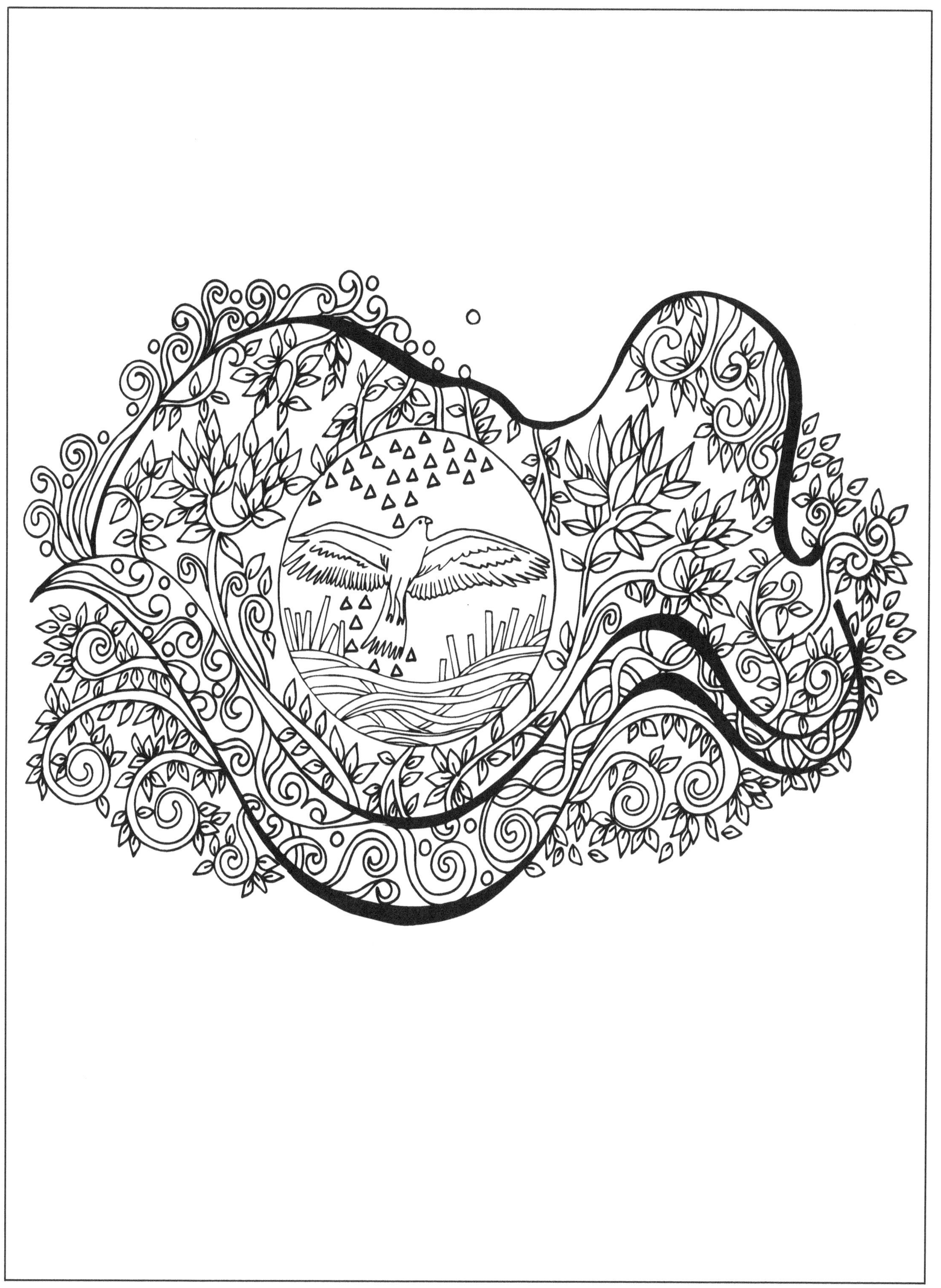

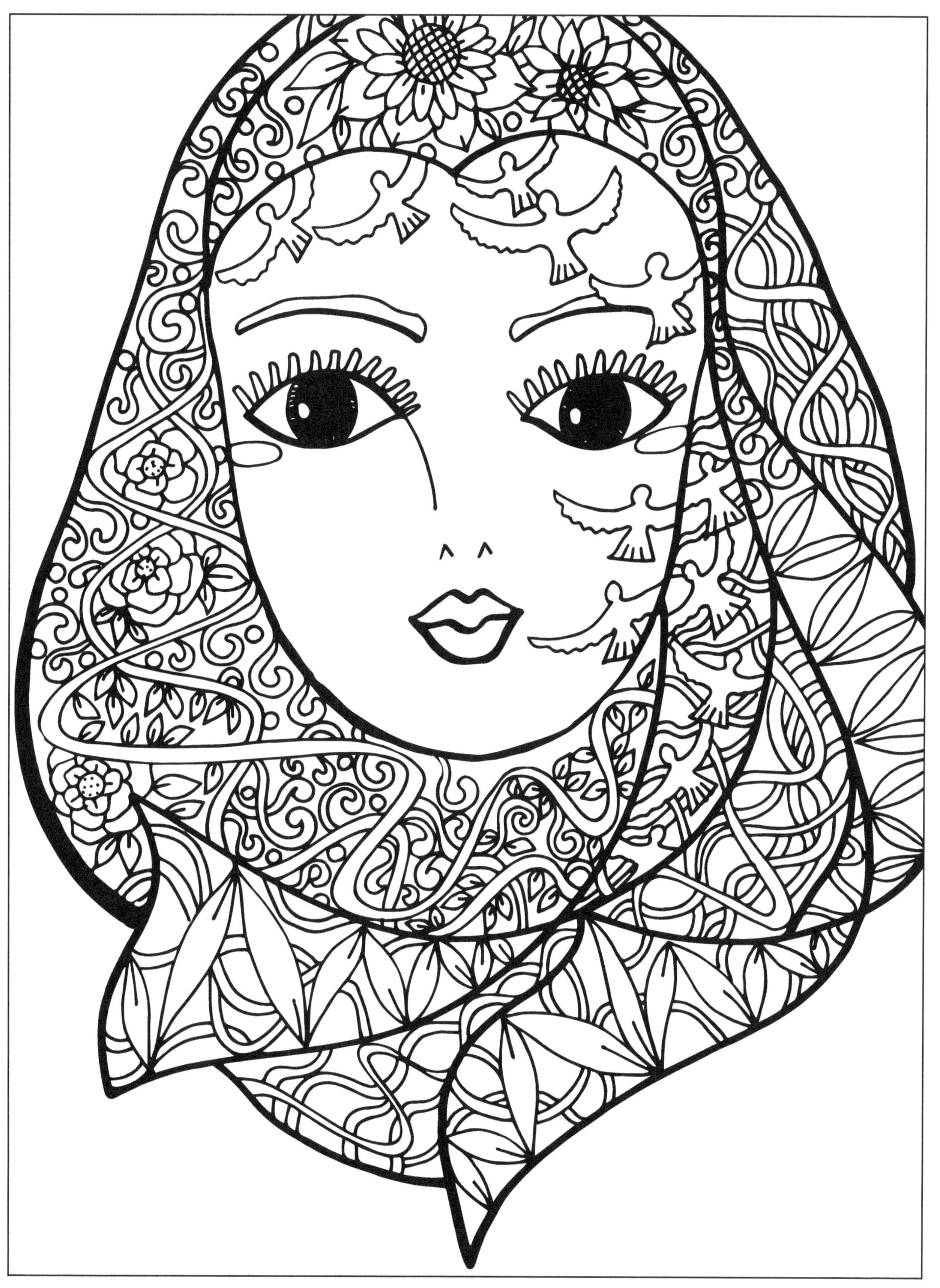

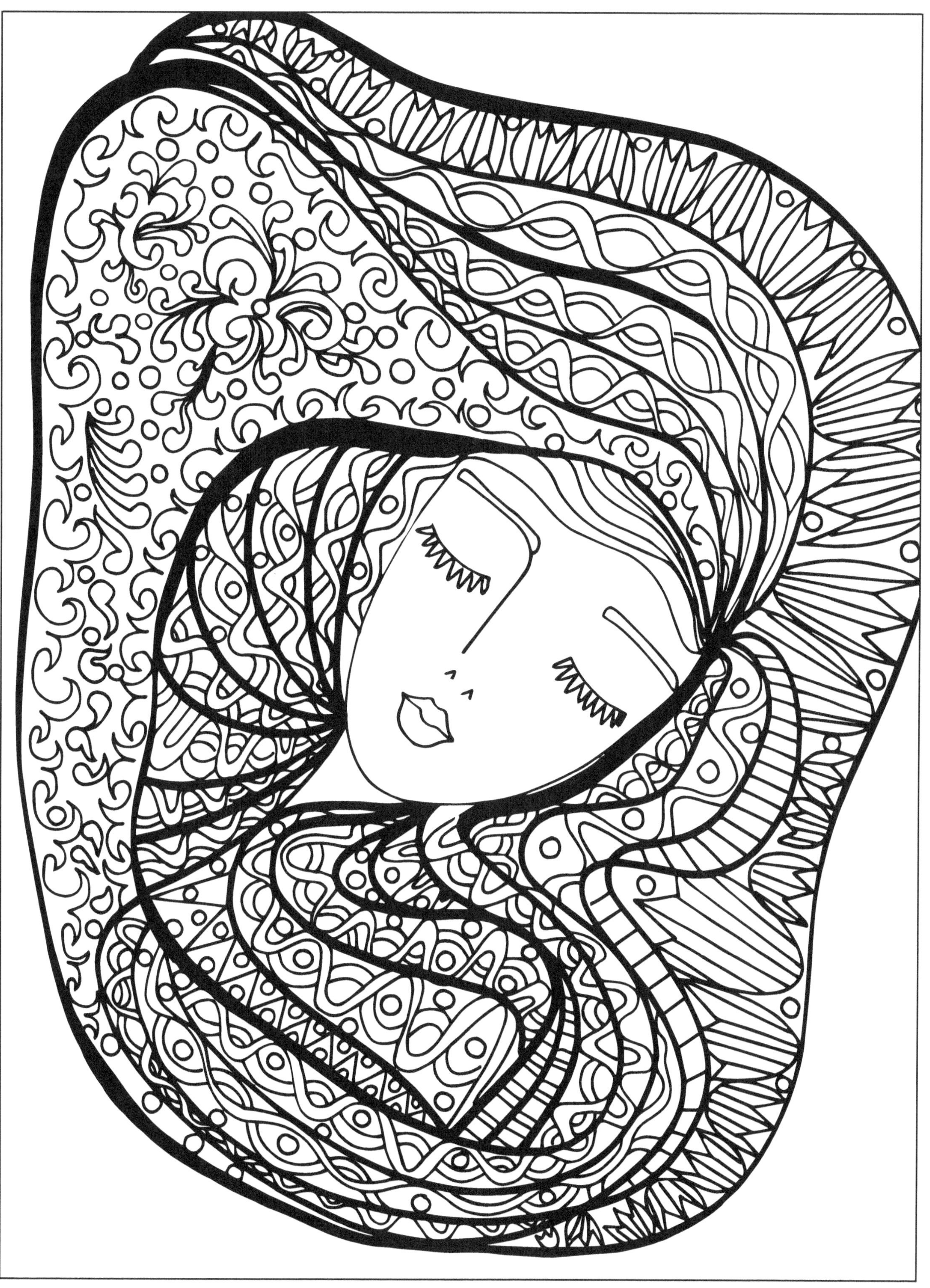

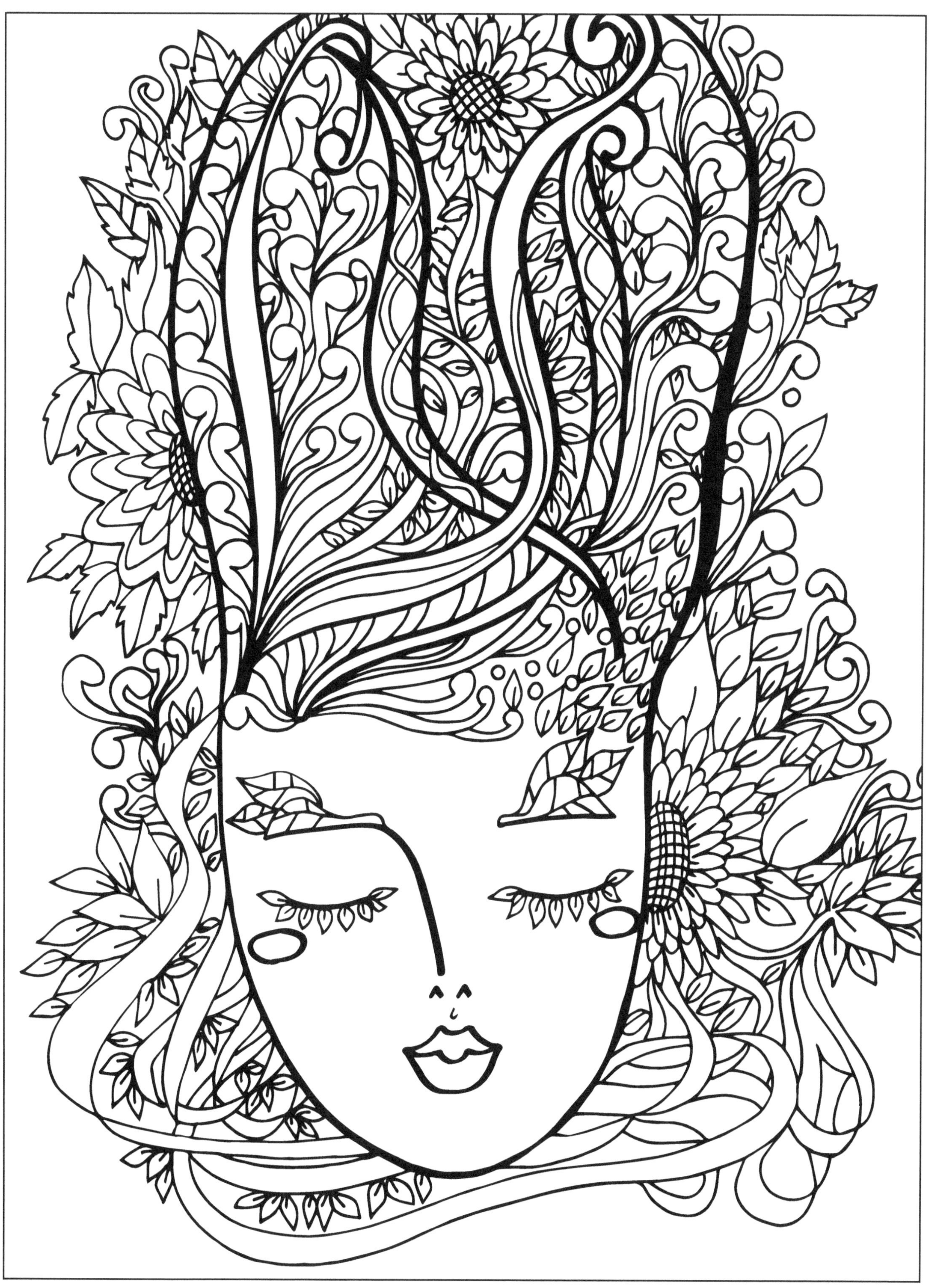

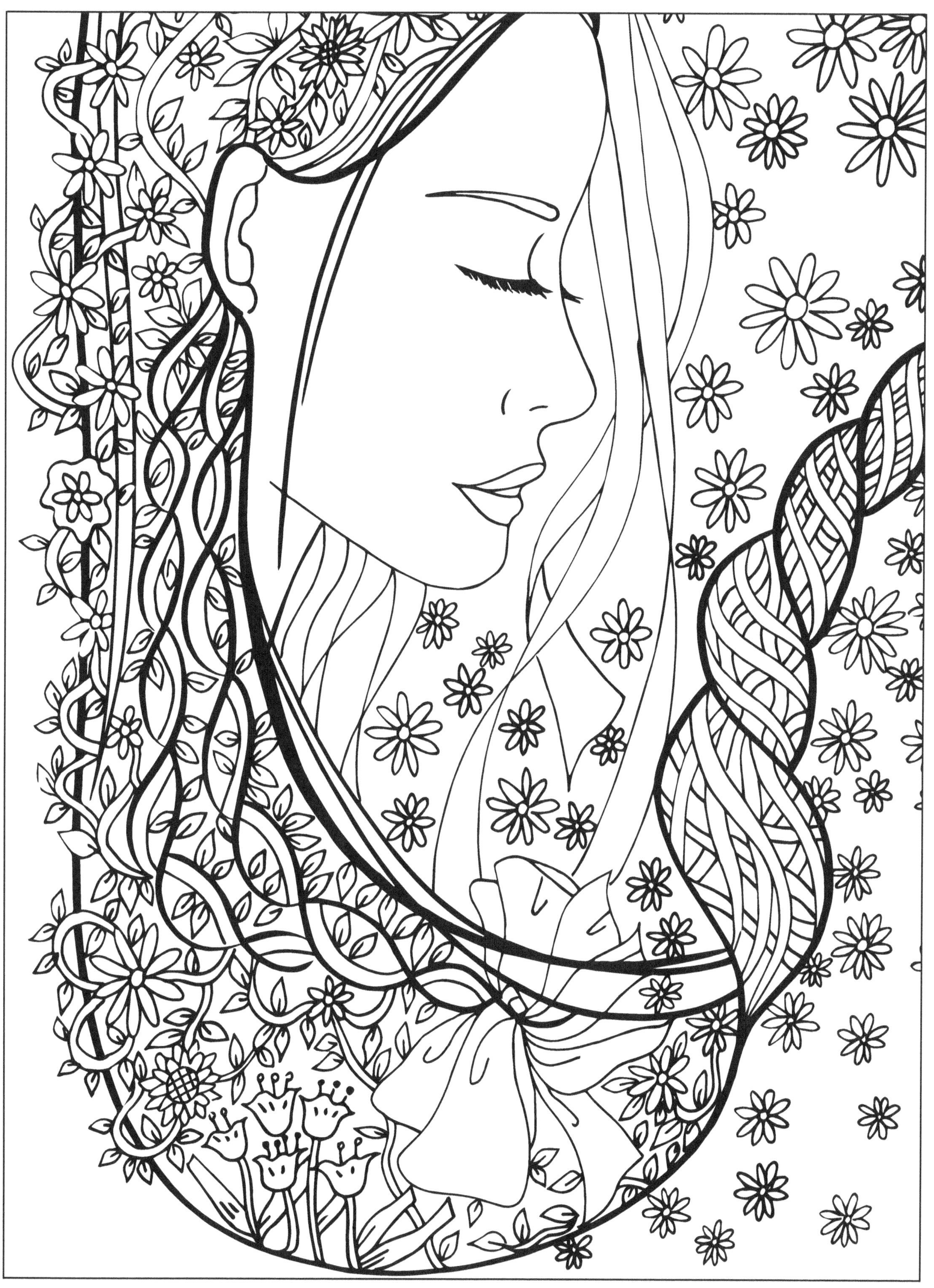

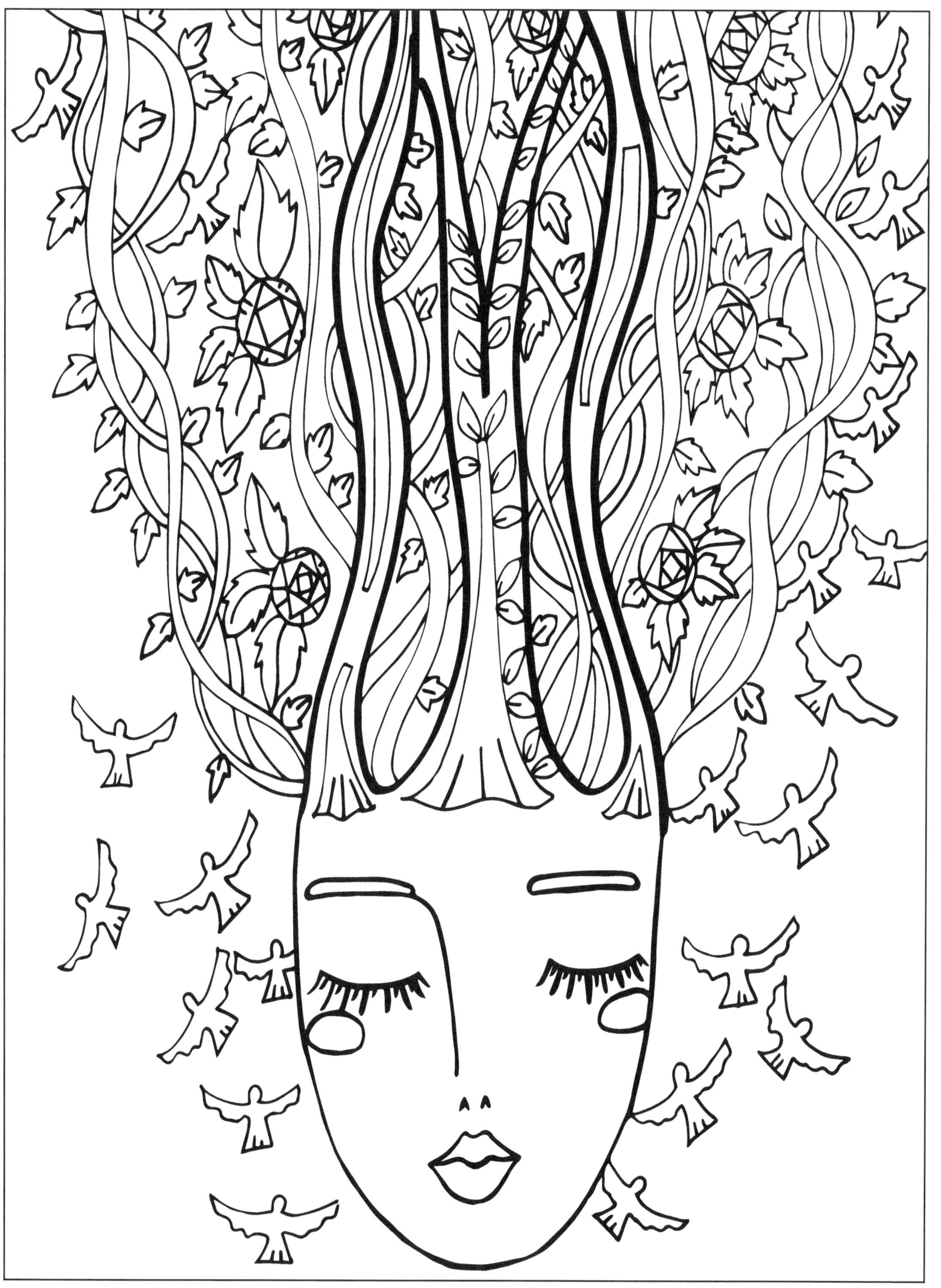

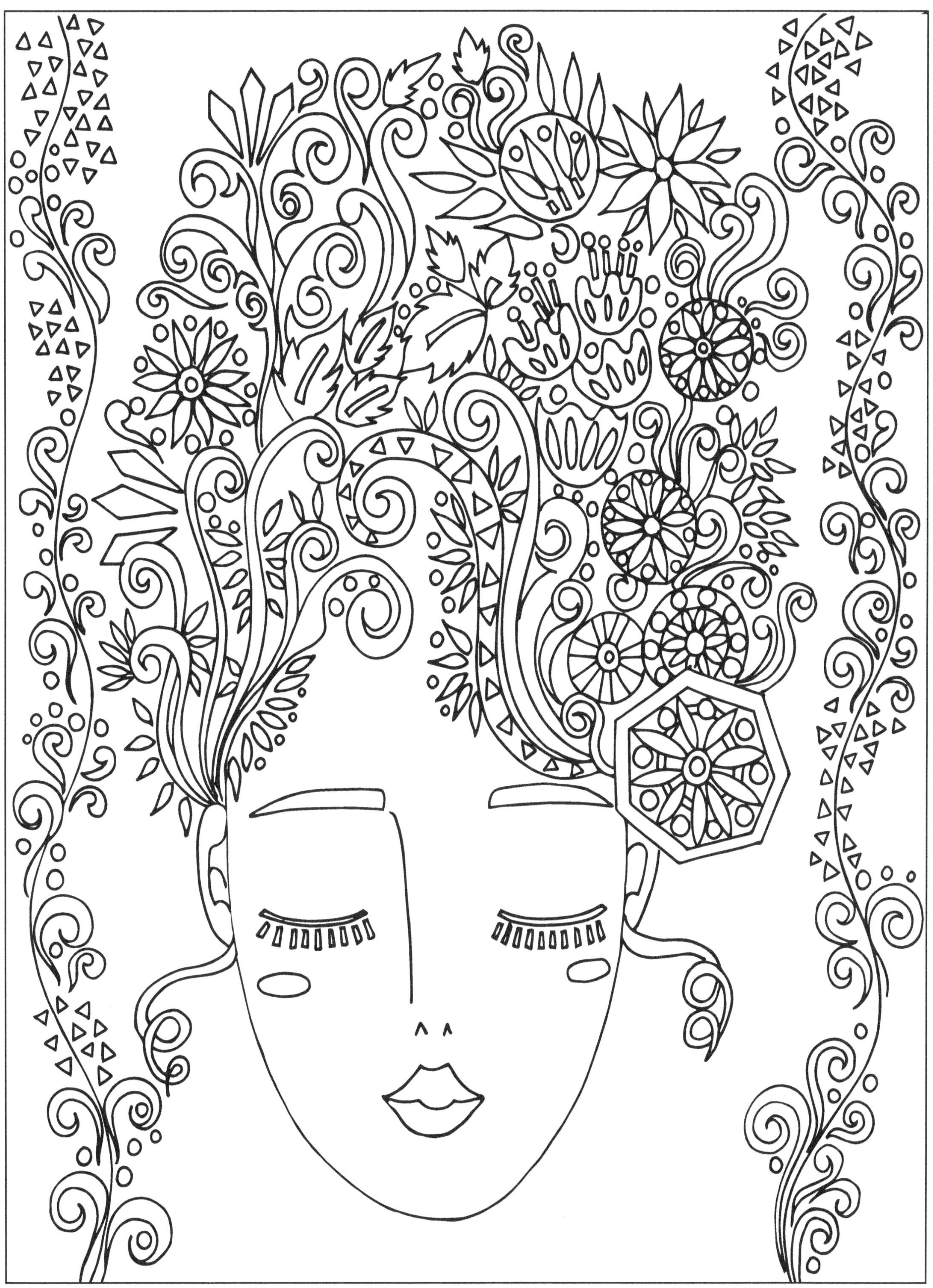

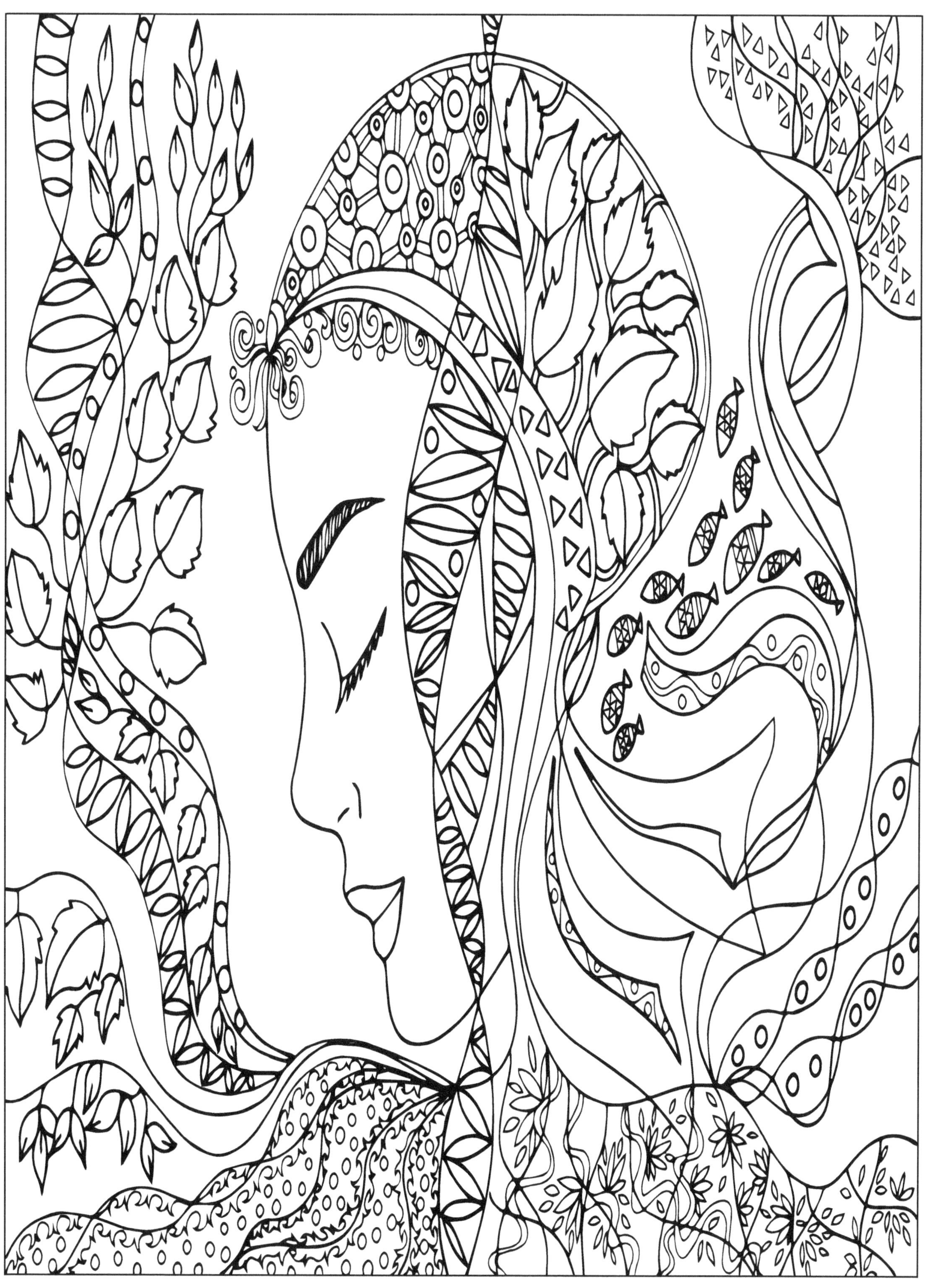

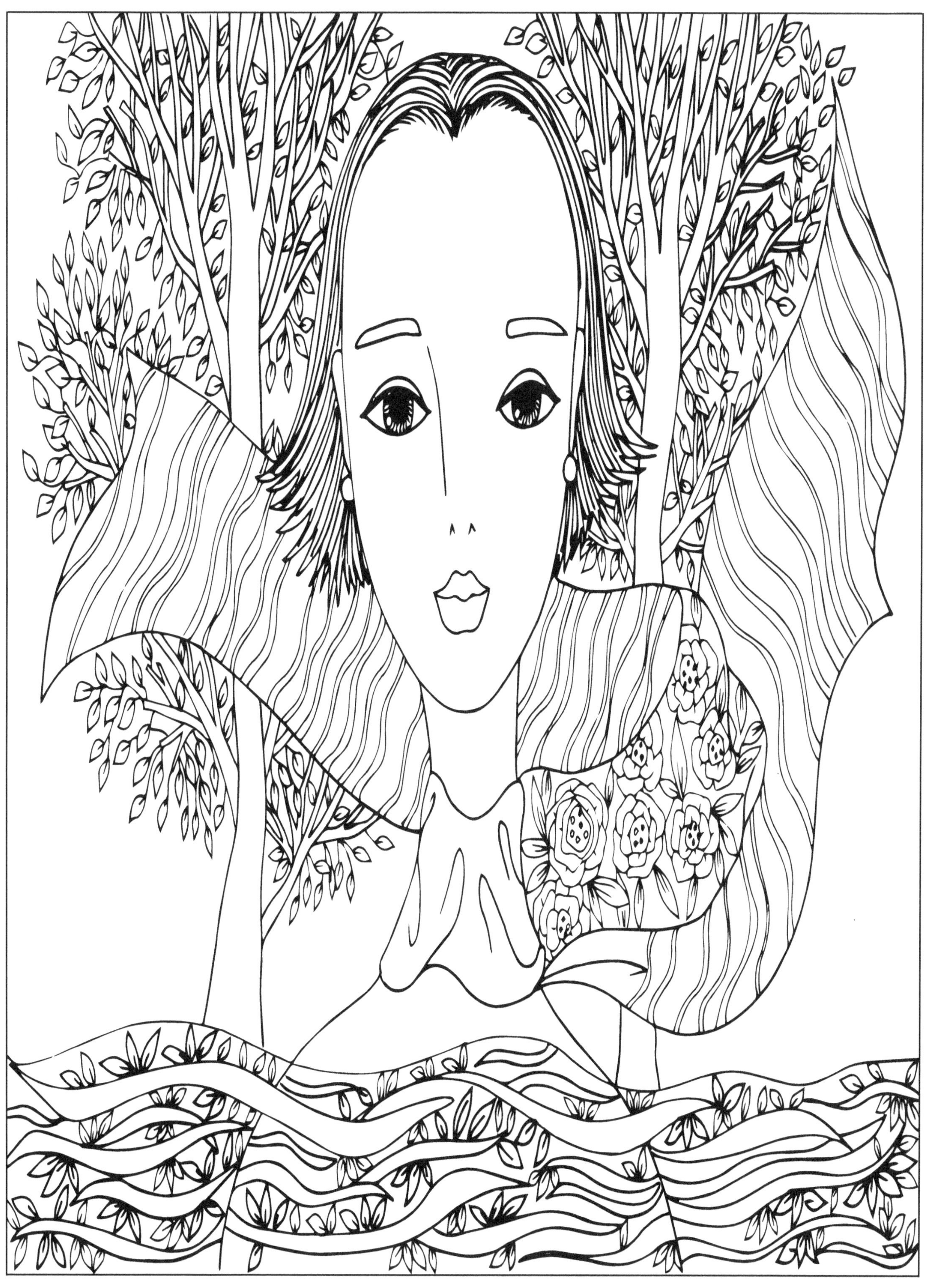

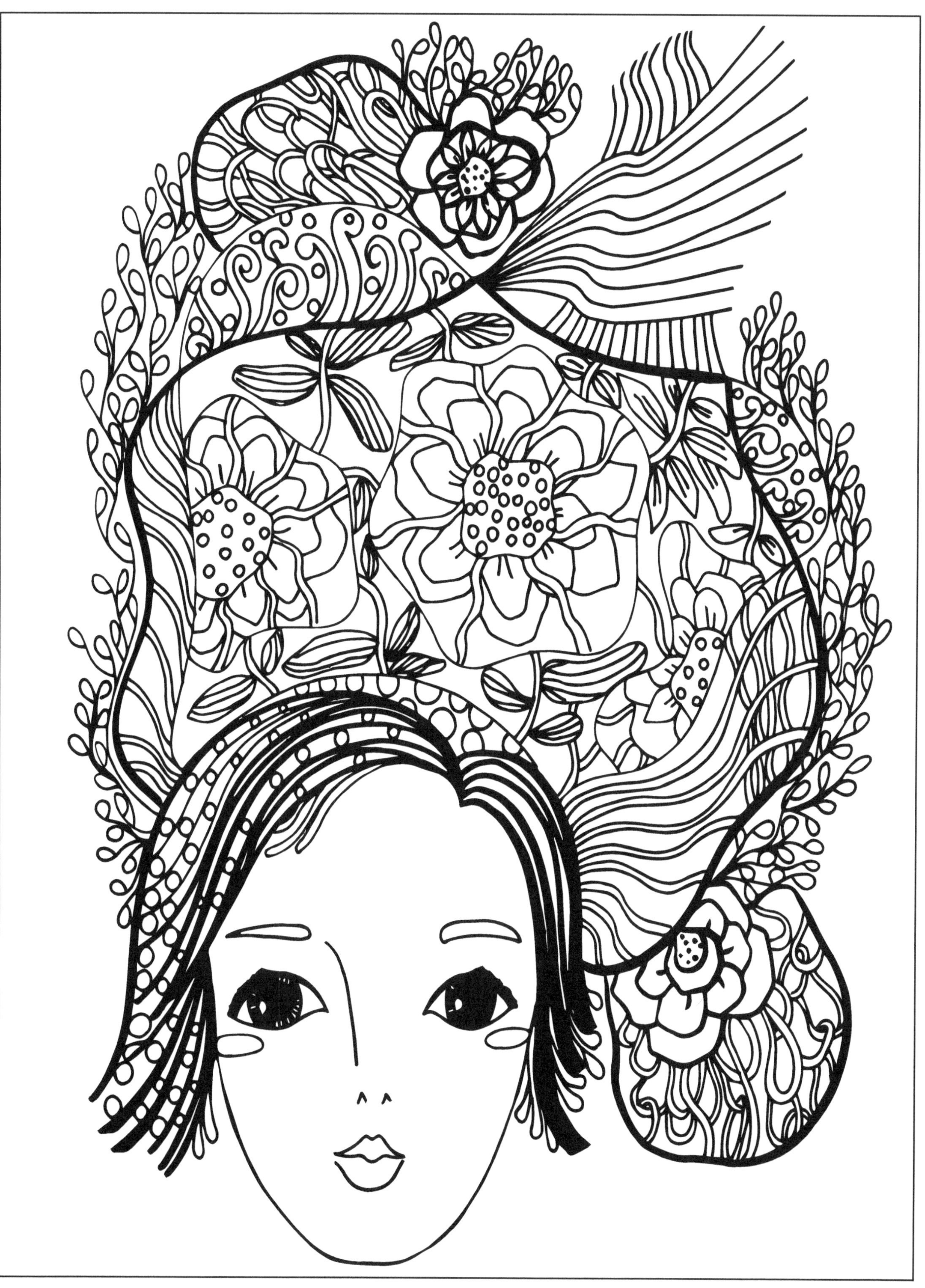

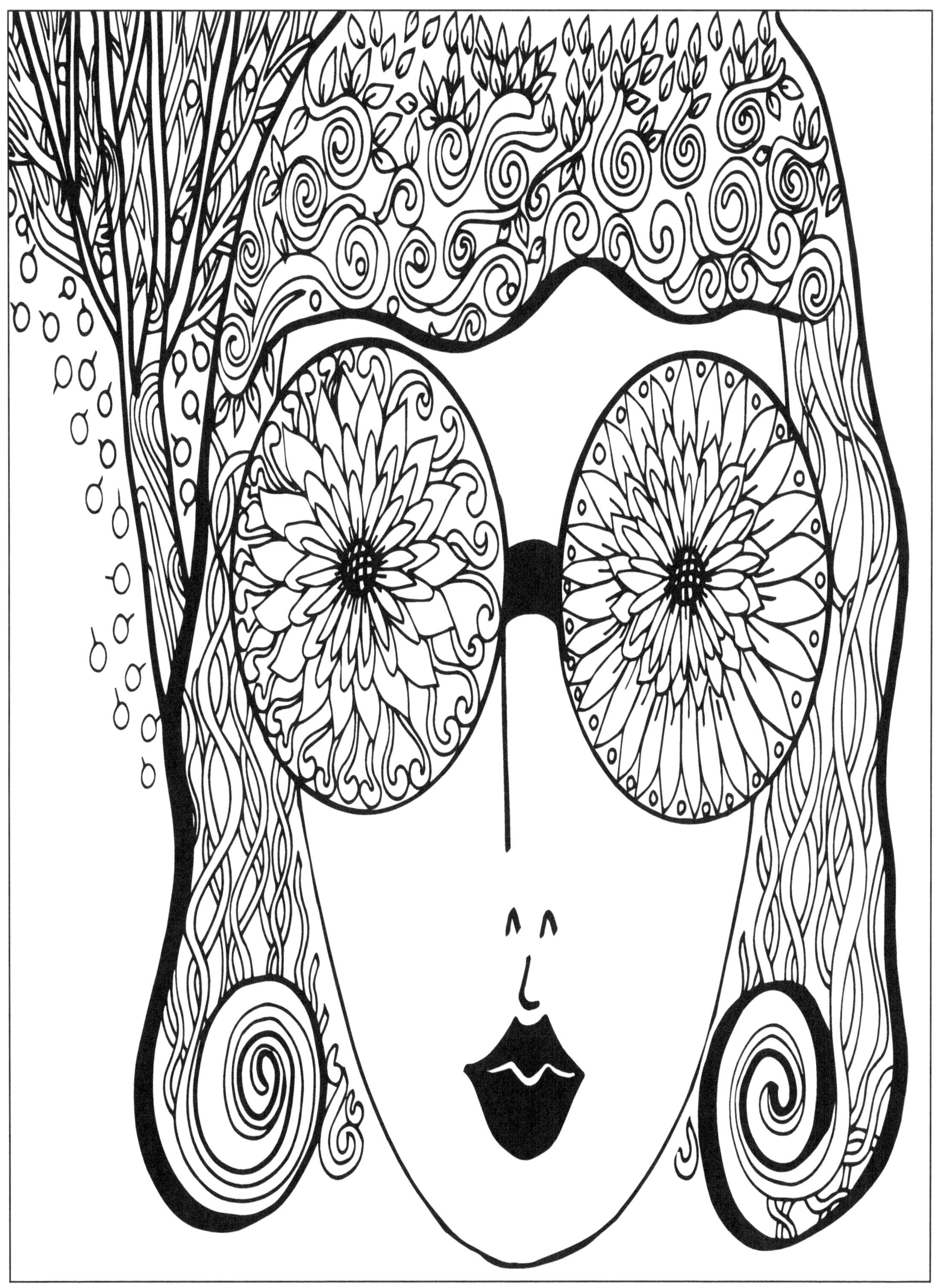

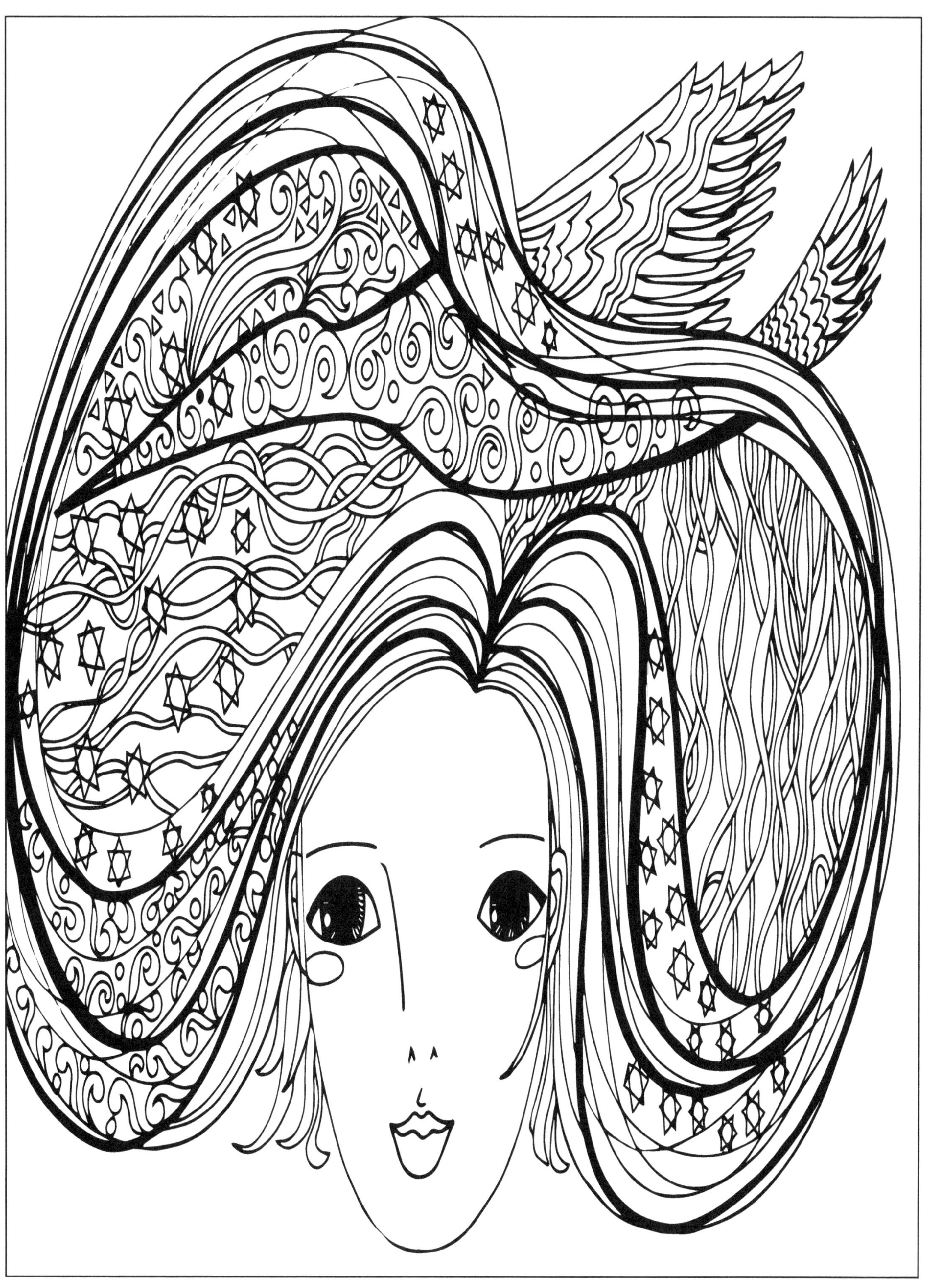

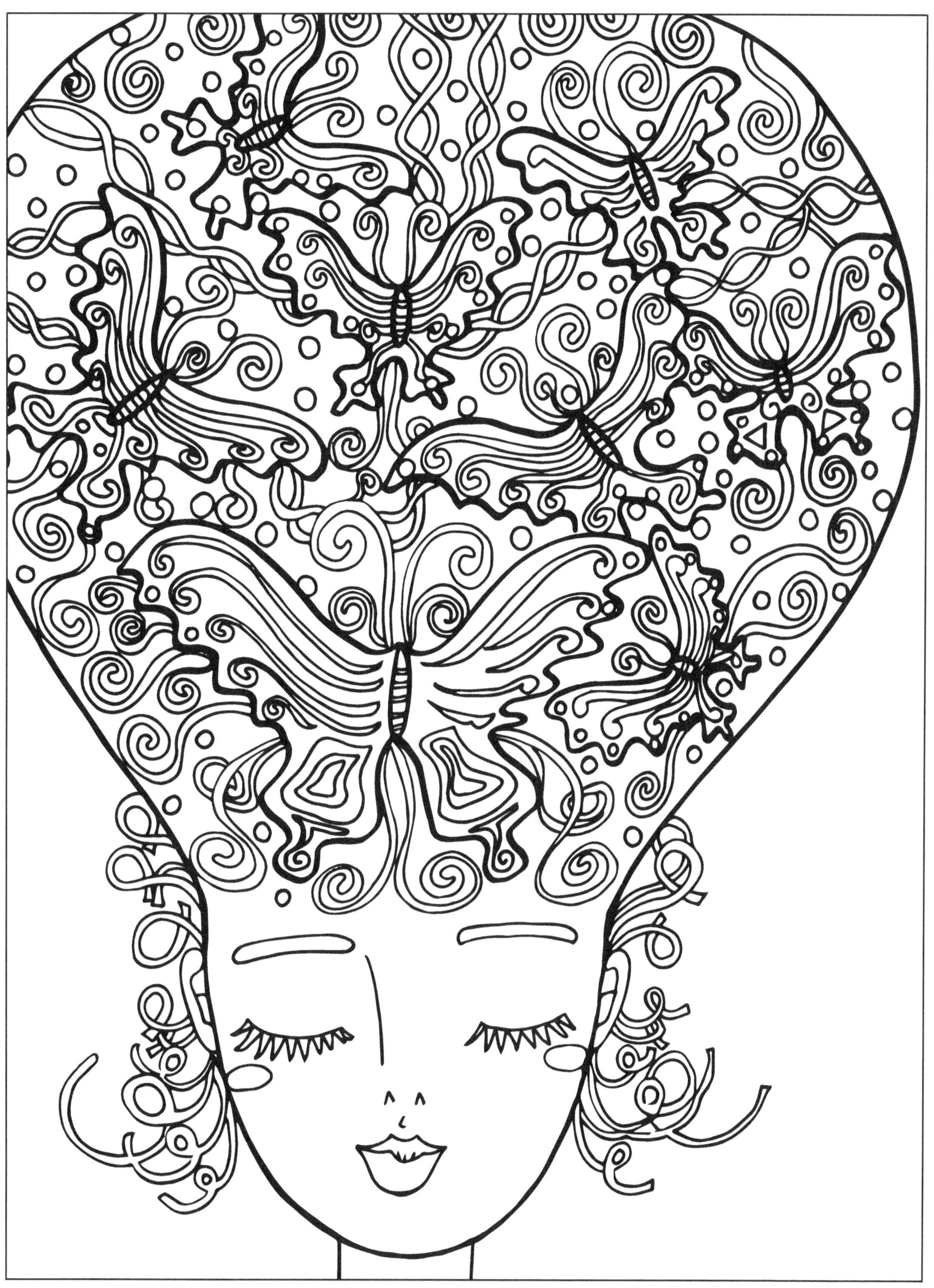

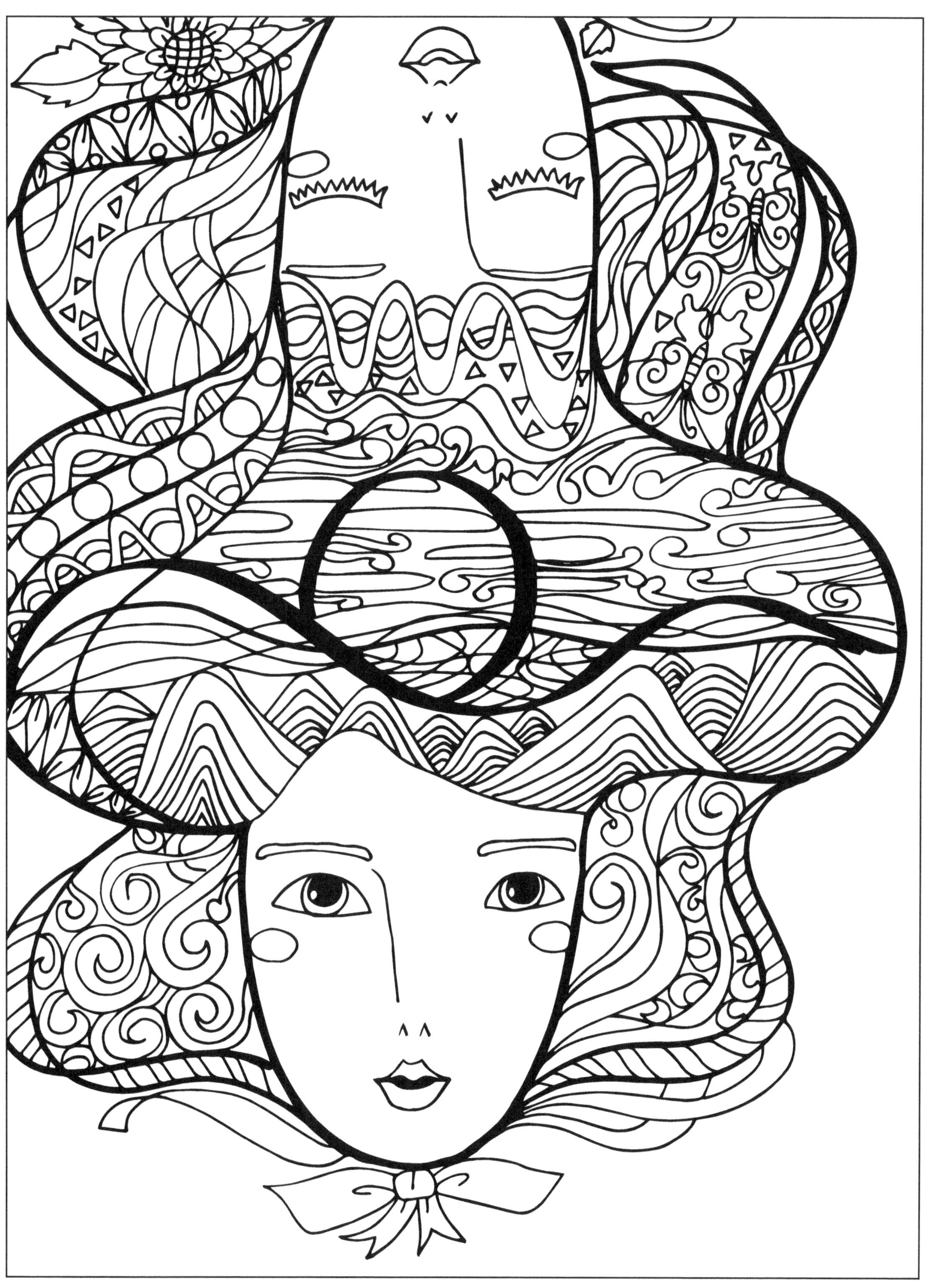

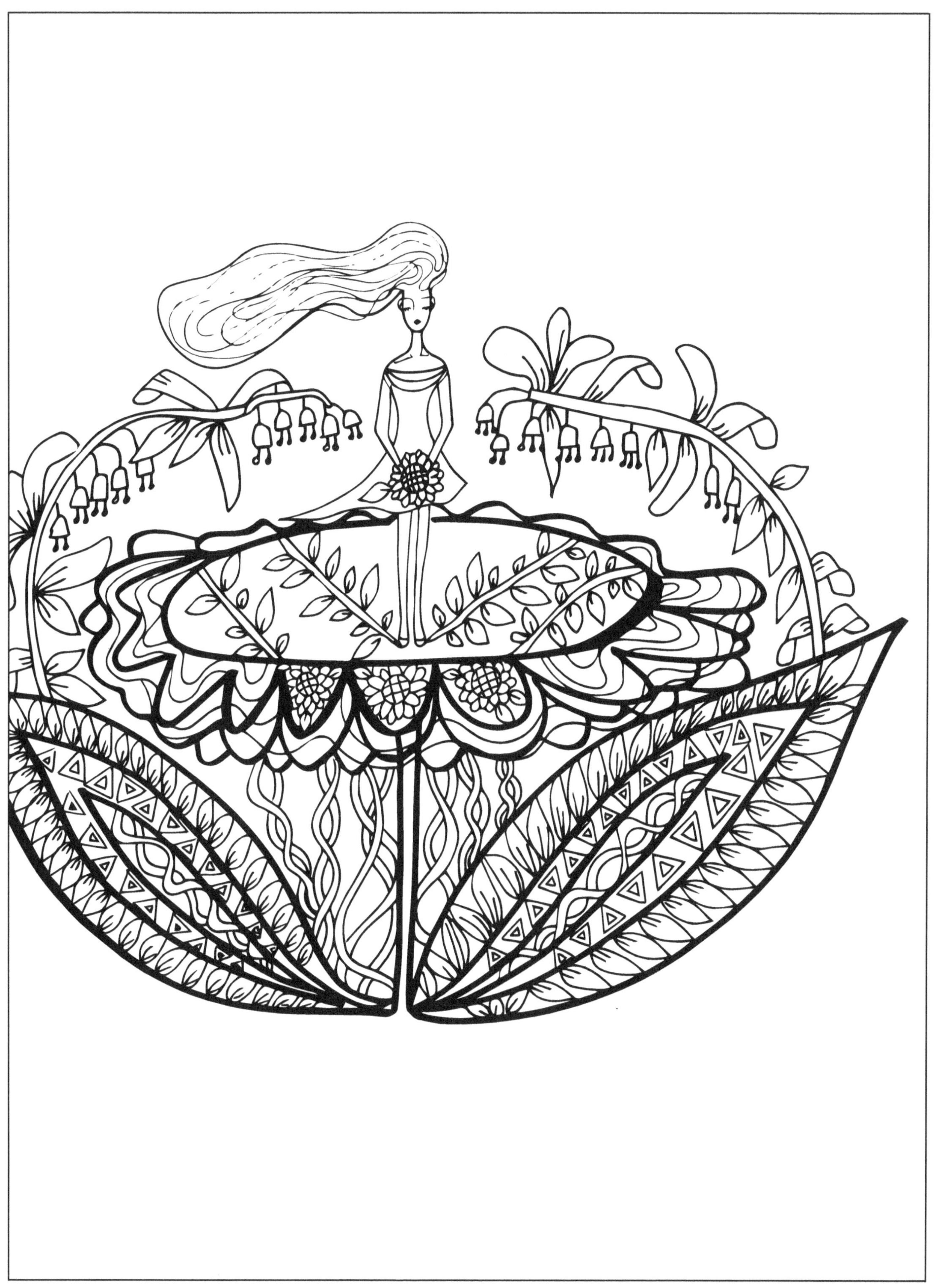

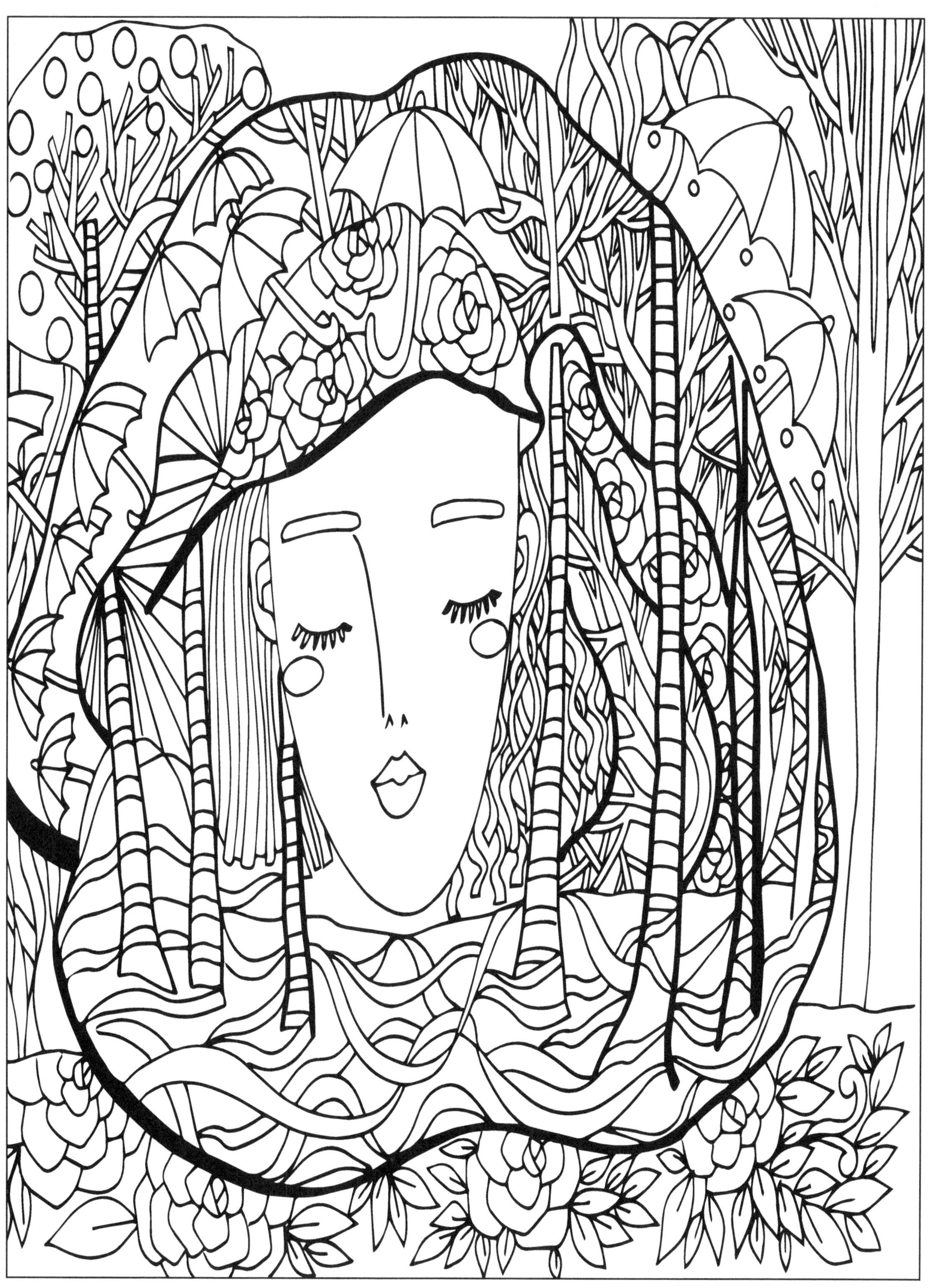

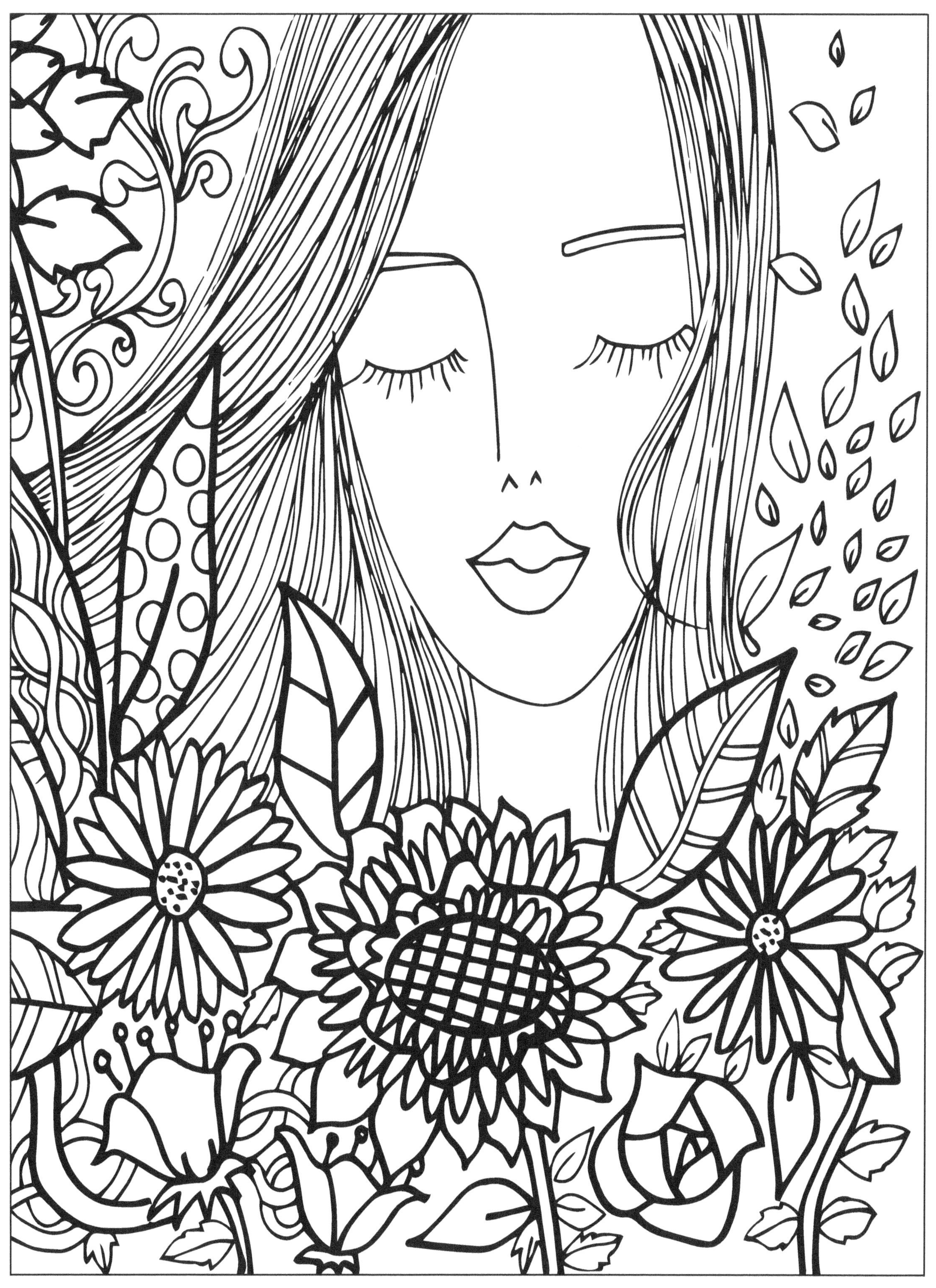

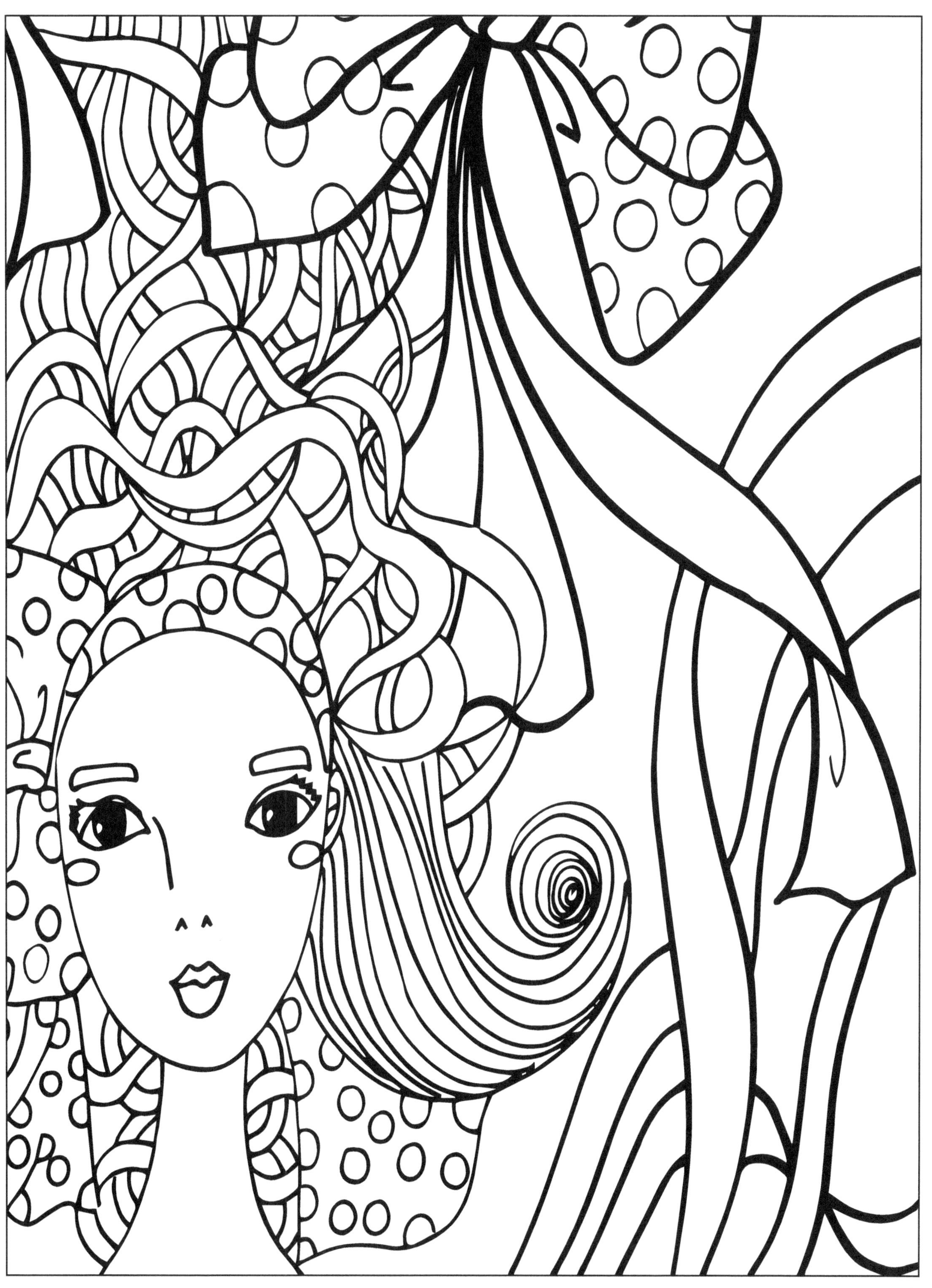

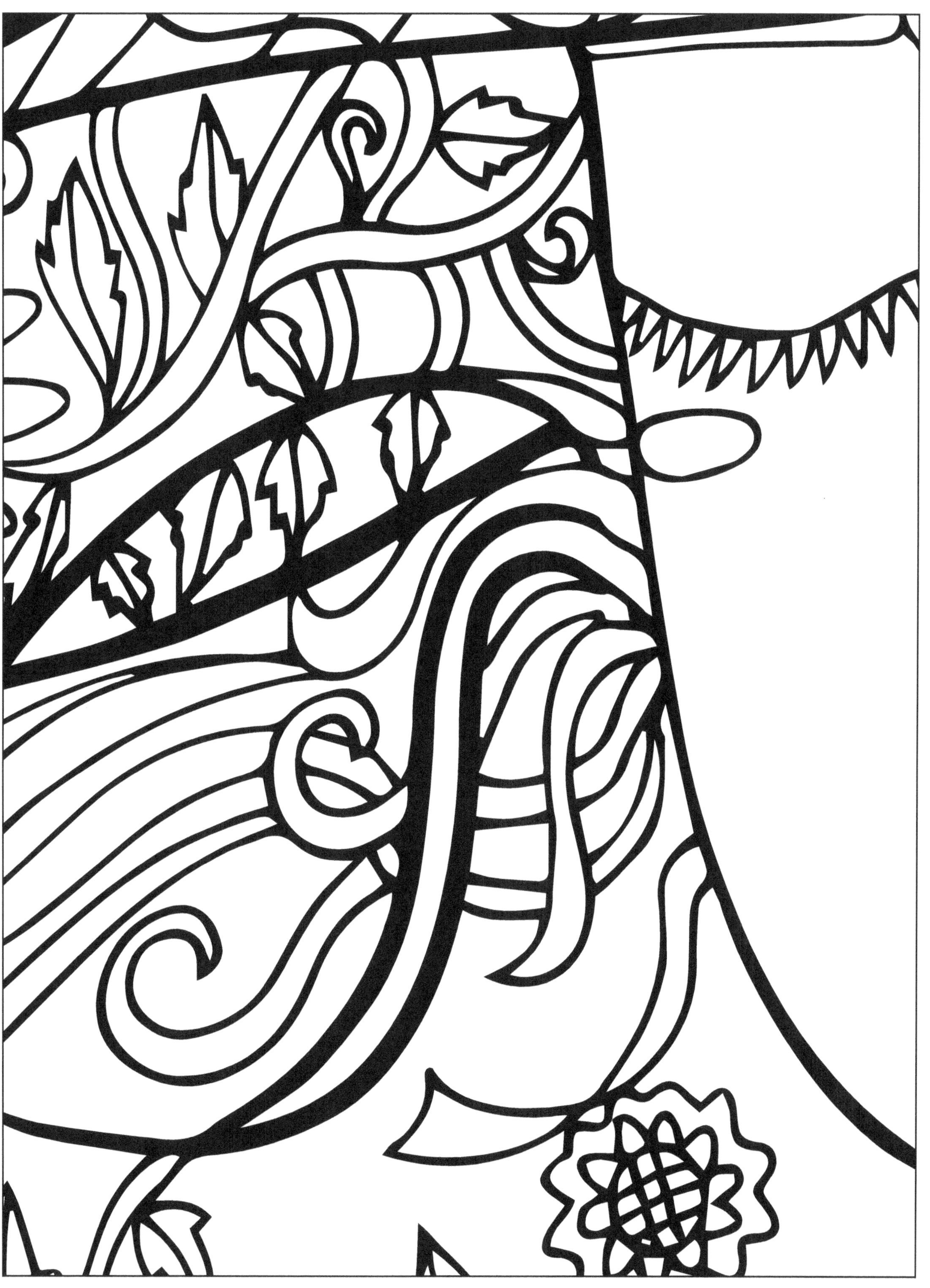

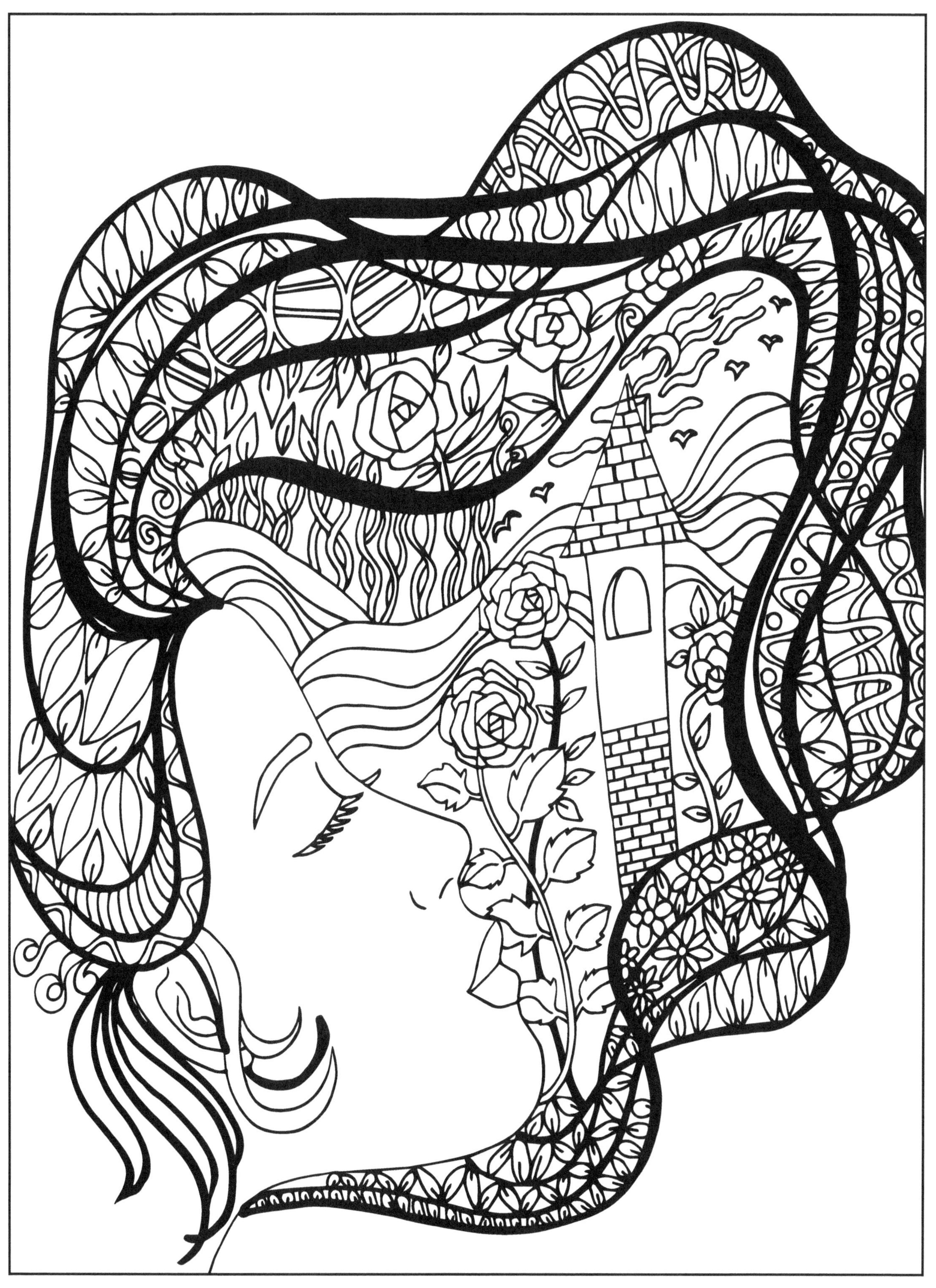